HIDDEN
HISTORY
of
EUREKA
SPRINGS

HIDDEN HISTORY

HISTORY

of

EUREKA SPRINGS

JOYCE ZELLER

Charleston · London

THE
History
PRESS

Published by The History Press
Charleston, SC 29403
www.historypress.net

All images are by the author unless otherwise noted.

First published 2011

Manufactured in the United States

ISBN 978.1.60949.376.9

Library of Congress Cataloging-in-Publication Data
Zeller, Joyce.
Hidden history of Eureka Springs / Joyce Zeller.
p. cm.
Includes bibliographical references.
ISBN 978-1-60949-376-9
1. Eureka Springs (Ark.)--History. 2. Eureka Springs (Ark.)--Biography. 3. Eureka Springs
(Ark.)--Social life and customs. 4. Historic buildings--Arkansas--Eureka Springs. 5. Eureka
Springs (Ark.)--Buildings, structures, etc. I. Title.
F419.E8Z45 2011
976.7'17--dc23
2011031488

Notice: The information in this book is true and complete to the best of our knowledge. It is
offered without guarantee on the part of the author or The History Press. The author and
The History Press disclaim all liability in connection with the use of this book.

Contents

PROLOGUE

Eureka Springs, Arkansas, is an accidental town that owes its existence to a chance encounter in the woods. Most towns begin for a reason—a crossroads or a trading post—but this curious hamlet owes its existence to a small puddle of water at the bottom of a hill and the rare chance that the right people happened by at the right time to make a difference. How else can you explain a settlement in deep, virtually uninhabited forest, with no roads leading to it, growing, in three months, to a population of twelve thousand?

This little hamlet, in the western half of Carroll County, northeastern Arkansas, right below the Missouri border, doesn't fit into an area that is traditionally southern in custom and 90 percent agricultural. The county is split in half by the Kings River, which flows north, when all other Arkansas rivers flow south, an indication that perhaps other things here aren't done in the usual way.

Eureka Springs, Arkansas, for more than a century, has, amid confusion and political chaos, maintained its reputation as a healing place while remaining one of the most politically cantankerous small towns in America. The town's role in the order of things has always been one of refuge and escape from the too harsh realities of life, and it still fulfills that need for visitors. It has been a safe haven since the beginning, the place where the walking wounded come for healing and renewal. It offers to travelers the peace they need in a nineteenth-century setting that is akin to a time warp. There are no modern shopping malls, no traffic lights and no parking garages. The downtown buildings were built of local limestone between 1886 and 1905.

Residential neighborhoods are made up of Victorian gingerbread cottages shaded by urban forest. The visitor's first impression is of an old town built in a ravine and clinging precariously to two sides of a mountain.

Aging Eureka Springs is the only surviving example of middle-class Victorian life in the United States and, as such, is declared of national significance by the National Register of Historic Places.

The citizens of this hamlet, home now to about 2,200 inhabitants, give little thought to modern fashion and even less to appearances. They regard laws as suggestive guidelines. They aren't concerned with how things should get done, only that they do, and in their own unique way.

Consider that a few years ago, in a fit of pique, they elected a dead woman to the city council. She was a former mayor who died unexpectedly after the deadline for filing, and the town didn't like the other candidate for the position. Then there was the matter of a former mayor posing nude—the interesting parts were behind a rock—for the cover of a national magazine. For yet another mayor in the 1960s, it was a point of pride to claim that during his reign aggravated citizens filed more lawsuits against him than any other mayor in the town's history. In 2008, some reactionary citizens sued the city council for installing parking meters in a parking lot.

In 2006, while Arkansas, which is considered a religious conservative state, was passing a constitutional amendment barring same-sex marriage, Eureka Springs established, by unanimous vote of the city council, a wildly controversial Domestic Partner Registry. This document officially recognizes cohabitation without marriage among common law and same-sex couples. It was a way to make dependent children in those relationships eligible for employer health benefits, but it created massive uproar across the country. City council members, before the final vote, were subjected to hundreds of e-mails from religious groups all over the world demanding they reject the idea. The vote, of course, was unanimously accepted. Later, the town successfully killed an effort by the state legislature, spearheaded by their own state representative, to make it illegal. To this day, it is the only town in Arkansas to offer health benefits to domestic partners of public employees.

No doubt you could blame all this contrariness on something in the water. That's reasonable, considering that's how the whole thing got started.

ACKNOWLEDGEMENTS

Discovering the hidden history of Eureka Springs required the sincere interest of many people, if only for conversation. Many thanks to all for their efforts.

Research, of course, is the backbone of any history. Thank you to the staff of the Eureka Springs Carnegie Library for their patience and research help: Christina Danas, Paul Harris, Kate Zakar, Loretta Crenshaw and Sarah Wright.

I owe a debt of gratitude to Ginni Miller, the director of the Eureka Springs Historical Museum, for finding all those bits and pieces of facts that added to the story.

Thanks to John Fuller Cross for being available to me to talk about his grandfather, Claude Fuller, and relating stories only he knew and making the vast collection of the Cornerstone Bank photographs available to me.

Thank you to Steve Reding of Videoland and Candy Doty of Penguin Graphics for rescuing this severely electronically disadvantaged writer from computer meltdown.

Thank you to Glenna Booth, the town historian, and Morris Pate, mayor of Eureka Springs.

Finally, to the Arkansas Ridgewriters, Dusty Richards, Velda Brotherton and the rest of the gang. I couldn't have done this without you.

It All Began
with a Puddle

The Ozark Mountain region of northwest Arkansas existed for thousands of years as dense woodland rich with animals and sparsely populated by the Osage Indians, who claimed as their own all the land in this region and southern Missouri. They repeated a tale told by the Cherokee about a healing spring located somewhere in the mountains west of the "Father of Waters," the Mississippi River. The legend told of a great Indian princess who had been cured of blindness and "great pain-in-the-bones" by bathing in the magic waters of this spring. Holding the ground sacred, they never revealed the location.

The legend spread throughout Europe. The Spanish explorer Ponce de Leon found documents on his uncle's ship telling of a healing spring in the new land that, if drunk and used for bathing, would cure ills the "Great Spirit intended to be cured." Indians throughout America knew of this spring, and Spanish coins dated in the fifteenth century, as well as other evidence, give credence that this was the Fountain of Youth sought by the explorer. He never found it.

In 1825, the Osage ceded the land to the United States government. It became part of the Louisiana Purchase, thus making it subject to the Federal Homestead Act, and was opened to white settlers. Before long, attracted by the abundant game, hunting parties from Berryville, fourteen miles west on the other side of the Kings River, began visiting the region and camping by a spring near the bottom of a ravine.

This very early photo of Basin Spring shows the site as it probably appeared when discovered by Alvah Jackson. The basin is about thirty-six inches across. *Courtesy of the Cornerstone Bank Collection.*

To understand how remote this area was in 1879, consider that Berryville, the only town of note in Carroll County, had 280 residents in 1880 when the first census was taken. The journey west to the spring took all day by horseback through deep forest, with a detour of several miles north in order to ford the Kings River. It wasn't until 1931 that a bridge was finally built across the Kings.

In 1854, Missourian Dr. Alvah Jackson and his son, who were hunting in the northwest corner of Arkansas, discovered the spring in a small, natural rock basin at the foot of a hill. For many years, Dr. Jackson had heard stories from the Osage Indians about "healing waters" flowing from a mountainside, but the location was unknown. He wondered if this might be it.

His son had been suffering for weeks from granulated eyelids, a chronic eye infection. On a hunch, Dr. Jackson camped by the spring and told his son to bathe his face in the water for a few days. The infection disappeared. The doctor, knowing a good thing when he saw it, took some of the water home with him and started selling it as a remedy for eye infections. Although business was brisk, he managed to keep the location of the spring a secret

Cave hospital.

until the Civil War ended in 1865, when he brought some wounded veterans to the site to help heal their wounds with the water. During their stay, they sought refuge in a cave above the spring, in the most primitive conditions imaginable. The cave is still there and easily seen, so small and inconvenient that one wonders how any healing could have occurred, but it did.

After the soldiers went home, the spring returned to obscurity until April 1879, when Dr. Jackson brought his friend Judge C. Burton Saunders of Berryville to the spring to cure his erysipelas, an extremely painful skin infection that had been plaguing him for months. To everyone's amazement, the persistent affliction began to heal. Judge Saunders decided to live by the spring until he was completely cured. He brought his wife and son, Buck, across the river, and they built a ten- by ten-foot cabin on the site, becoming the first residents.

Saunders's enthusiasm for the water spread by word of mouth, and fate intervened with one of her many twists. The news carried far from home. There was a healing spring in the woods of northwest Arkansas. The discovery became an overnight sensation.

To understand how rapidly the word could spread, consider the mood of the times. The Civil War, which in some pockets of the South is still referred to as the War of Northern Aggression, had ended in 1865, but the aftermath saw thousands of soldiers suffering from incurable bone infections manifested by painful, open sores, the inevitable result of bullet wounds and a lack of sterile surgical conditions. Antisepsis was still a theory and not yet accepted practice by the end of the Civil War.

The populace lived in fear of unexplainable illnesses that would strike at any time, without reason and with no hope for cure. Late nineteenth-century medicine was in a state somewhere between folklore, faith healing and superstition. A common illness, like cholera infantum, a severe bowel disorder, took the lives of many babies within hours.

"The Waste" or "Falling Away" was a mysterious, always fatal condition, in which the victim simply wasted away. In a book of remedies published in 1820 entitled *Pow-Wows on Arts and Remedies*, the author, John J. Hohman, demonstrates the state of medical knowledge only forty years before the time. He suggests a "remedy for Falling Away that has cured many persons": "Let the person in perfect soberness, who has not conversed with anyone catch rain in a pot, before sunrise; boil an egg in this; bore three holes with a needle and carry it to an ant hill; and the person will feel relieved as soon as the egg is devoured."

Moreover, virulent epidemics, like the yellow fever sickness that swept the lowlands along the Mississippi River in 1878, left twenty thousand dead and people fleeing the delta, looking for relief, in search of higher ground. With a feeling that traditional medicine was failing them, the people embraced any idea that offered hope. People living with constant, chronic pain wanted to feel better, even for a few hours. Desperate for a miracle, they flocked to any location rumored to be curative: hot springs, spas here and abroad or simply clean mountain air. By 1879, the country was ready for news of a healing haven. It is understandable that word of a healing spring would spread like wildfire.

The wonder of it all was that the pilgrims managed to find it. The road to the spring was uncharted, and the terrain housing the spring was inaccessible. Impenetrable woods, snakes, boars and bears were no deterrent to the determined. There were primitive trails, merely wagon tracks, barely paths in the woods, but the afflicted followed them and somehow arrived at their destination.

Covered wagons camped around Basin Spring early in May 1879. *Courtesy of the Cornerstone Bank Collection.*

By July 1879, there were twenty families—about four hundred people—camped at the site. They had thrown up tents or shacks around the spring, tethered their horses and oxen nearby and bathed in the water. The spring emerged from the mountain higher up and flowed into the stone basin. It is assumed that the uphill source was used for drinking. Stories of miraculous cures grew in number every day.

The new settlers had a common bond. Shared pain and desperation brought these people together in a spirit of cooperation and camaraderie. They needed to identify this place in the wilderness and find a name for the spring, so they held a meeting. A lot of suggestions emerged from the crowd, like "Saunders's Spring," but according to L.J. Kalklosch, a local resident who would become historian of the town, a Mr. McKay, enjoying his two minutes of fame, suggested "Eureka!" Greek for "I've found it." The exclamation is attributed to Archimedes, a scholar in ancient Greece who discovered the displacement theory of solids to liquid while sitting in a tub of water. With a roar of approval, the name was accepted, and a town was born.

An example of an early log home built by the first settlers in Eureka Springs. Notice the dimensions of probably twelve feet square and the number of family members housed there. One of the original cabins has been preserved and is outside the Eureka Springs Museum downtown. *Courtesy of the Cornerstone Bank Collection.*

Kalklosch commented wryly: "The absurdity of building a city in such a place with no inducement but the water, was talked of by many."

It didn't take long for things to get out of hand. By the end of the summer, there were several thousand people camped haphazardly around the spring, with only five hundred houses minimally able to withstand the coming winter, but still they came in droves.

Consider the ordeal of getting here. There were no roads, only rutted wagon tracks. The closest train was eighteen miles to the north at Seligman, Missouri. From there, the journey took five agonizing hours. For the sick and injured, it meant enduring misery in a wagon rocking over deep ruts in a barely visible path through the woods.

Cora Pinckley-Call, descended from the original residents, describes the sight of this remarkable migration in her book *Frontier Tales*, published in 1930.

> *Standing at the top of East Mountain and looking toward the spring, one*
> *can hear the lowing of cattle and the neigh of horses, the braying of donkeys*
> *and mules. As people pour down the mountainside you hear the screams and*
> *groans from the suffering as the wagons bounce and jostle over the rocks and*

the ill-made road. They carry them down the mountain on stretchers, in chairs, in their arms—every which way.

By April of the following year, the population was estimated to be fifteen thousand. Building continued at a wild pace, denuding the surrounding hills of lumber. Each settler who staked his claim immediately took to cutting down the trees without any thought of conservation. The price paid for this carelessness was the frequent mudslides.

Boardinghouses and primitive shacks were built anywhere there was a scrap of vacant land, but since there were no legal boundaries or lot lines, no one was entirely sure who owned what. There were no streets, so houses faced any direction.

The newcomers wanted security. They needed to know the land they lived on was theirs. They were depending on the Federal Homestead Act to legitimize their claim. The act decreed that any man could file a claim to

Circa 1880 view of the hill behind Basin Spring, covered in shacks and completely devoid of trees, adding to the mud problem at the bottom of the hill. *Courtesy of the Cornerstone Bank Collection.*

a piece of surveyed land, get a receipt for payment of one dollar, put up a dwelling, live there and the land was his, as long as he built an "improvement," but there were no surveys upon which to file a claim.

It was time for a leader to step forth and get things organized in the fledgling community.

The Birth of a Town

O ne of the first volunteers to emerge was Hugh Montgomery, a man about whom little is known except that there was a Montgomery Brothers Mercantile established about that time. He must have been a first-class organizer. With a group of about a dozen friends, he led the effort to clear some land of brush and debris in the gully at the base of the hill, below the spring, so some businesses could be built. This makeshift road was to become Main Street, today known as Highway 23. It ran alongside a creek that flooded frequently, and during heavy rain, mud would settle there from the barren slopes, so the thoroughfare quickly became "Mud Street."

It's not hard to imagine what would have happened if Montgomery hadn't stepped forward and taken the reins. Eureka Springs was overwhelmed with outsiders, realizing the profit potential from the rumors of miraculous cures, determined to claim ownership of all the springs for themselves. Land barons greedy for the timber and the sawmill business, speculators eager to make money off rumored mineral riches and opportunists seeing profits if all the properties were secured were claiming rights to every scrap of land.

Unknown to the locals, a pair of speculators from Missouri, Messrs. Northcutt and Alexander, anticipating a fortune to be made from the fame of the healing water, filed homestead claims for any land that included a spring. Considering that there are sixty-two known springs in the area today, it's not hard to grasp the magnitude of the problem. The original documents are lost, so there is no way of knowing how many claims were filed. The men were referred to as "the agriculturalists" because of the nature of their claim.

Montgomery realized the need for some legal order, so in October 1879, he gathered twenty signatures to petition the Carroll County Court, in Berryville, for the power to incorporate as a town. His leadership abilities got all the townsfolk working with him. In the early days of the settlement, what would later become a culture of dissent had not yet taken shape. People were too busy simply trying to survive.

The first petition was dismissed because there weren't enough qualified signatures. Undaunted, the citizens submitted a second petition seven days later, and incorporation was finally achieved on February 14, 1880. While waiting for their petition to be granted, Montgomery, his brother and ten others got themselves elected by the townsfolk as a committee. They would be the first governing body, or city council, of the soon-to-be town.

The first order of business was a survey. The committee appointed a Major Armstrong as the town surveyor, with orders to make lots forty by forty feet, streets thirty feet wide and eighty feet between streets. That early survey, with few modifications, stands today, which means there are major streets in Eureka Springs barely wide enough for a wagon to pass a buggy, with sharp, blind curves on two-way streets wide enough for only one car and steep grades.

Eager would-be residents followed Major Armstrong around while he worked. As soon as he had a lot surveyed, they paid their dollar, got a receipt and had their name recorded in a book. No party could buy more than two lots, to guard against speculation.

By the end of 1879, 1,500 lots had been surveyed; however, there was a problem. The indomitable L.J. Kalklosch explains the situation with humor in his book *The History of Eureka Springs*, published in 1881. He observes that the major was not always the trustworthiest of men. In this account, he describes the process:

> *The surveyor was always followed by parties ready to pay the fee and register the lots, so that it proved to be quite a bonanza for him, especially when we recollect that he frequently "received payment" and gave receipts for the same lot from one to three times. Owing to several claimants on the*

same lots, frequent disputes arose, and the Surveyor thought he knew of a healthier clime for him than Eureka Springs, but not until he had reaped a rich harvest.

Growth continued unabated. By 1881 the estimate of business activity was fifty-seven boardinghouses, one bank, thirty-three groceries, twelve saloons, twelve real estate offices, twenty-two doctors and one undertaker.

Franzisca Massman, a very formidable lady who owned a lumberyard, might have outwitted them all. She was only interested in the trees, so she would file a claim. Unfortunately, some of her claims were filed on land that had already been filed on by someone else. She had to move quickly. Her crew would follow behind her and, the same day, cut down enough trees to build a shack. By evening, she would move in some furniture, have dinner, stay the night and thereby fulfill the homestead requirements. When she'd harvested all the trees, she'd move on. It was rumored that she carried all her money and a revolver with her in a black satchel as she drove her buggy around town.

Since Hugh Montgomery's committee had been given absolute power, they resolved disputes, usually in favor of the one with the earliest dated receipt. Their decision was never argued, but the problem didn't end there.

Although Eureka Springs was finally incorporated on February 14, 1880, the battle over ownership of the land went on for five more years. That May, the newly elected mayor, Elisha Rossen, made application for a town site, establishing boundaries for the town, at the land office in Harrison. Unfortunately, by the end of the summer, Mayor Rossen was accused of "gross improprieties" by the citizens and impeached.

As the fame of the water spread, so did the news of money to be made. That brought an influx of opportunists and an end to the carefree attitude of the town. Any lot in town could have as many as three owners. In addition to the locals, referred to as "settlers," and the aforementioned "agriculturalists," a third group, in response to rumors of minerals like zinc and silver in the area, created the Blue Springs Mining Company. They filed for the mineral rights in the town and immediately began prospecting for minerals. Outraged residents, finding men digging holes on what they considered their land, chased them off and filled in the holes, fearing their springs would be polluted with the digging. Blue Springs Mining sued

Alexander and Northcutt; however, the Harrison land office decided that some of the town was "mineral," and prospecting resumed.

The city council did manage to protect the springs by passing Ordinance 10, which made it against the law to wash persons or clothes in or above the springs and declared the springs free for public use with some exceptions: livestock could not be watered directly, nor could anything be destroyed. By now one might point out that enforcement could be made difficult because the city might not own the land, but the town thought the law was a good thing, regardless of the legality. A modern comparison might be our compliance with the law that requires all of us to drive in the same direction on the right-hand side of the road. One might contend that our civil rights, and perhaps freedom of expression, are being violated, but common sense prevails.

By 1881, the city had reached a population of more than five thousand, which qualified it to become a city of the first class, with more authority to govern. Oddly enough, the authority for the city to upgrade to city of the first class was received from the governor about the same time that the federal land office in Harrison refused to grant the town site application until all legal claims were solved. This meant that the battle still raged.

An election was held for a new council and mayor. Eureka Springs desperately needed a seasoned politician of great common sense to sort out

The Honorable John Carroll.

the financial and legal mess choking the city. The Honorable John Carroll was that man. He was elected mayor in the spring of 1881. The right man would save the infant city again just in time.

Colonel Carroll had served as an officer in the Confederacy until the end of the war, when he practiced law in Madison County, just south of Eureka. He was elected to the state legislature and served as a delegate to the state constitutional convention. In 1874, he retired and moved his law practice to Eureka Springs. He brought a level of experience in Arkansas politics that was needed at this time in the history of the new town.

Meanwhile, Powell Clayton, governor of Arkansas from 1868 to 1871, had been watching Eureka Springs. He was heavily invested in railroads and saw tremendous business opportunities in the development of the town if the right people were in charge. The Eureka Springs Improvement Company (ESIC), organized by Clayton in 1884 with three friends, joined Northcutt and Alexander, the agriculturalists, in the legal battle over the land. Clayton had purchased a home in Eureka in 1882 with an eye to development after becoming a resident.

They filed claims on lots in town around the springs. Members were railroad men and had plans for Eureka's development as a health resort. Clearly, they had unlimited funds and were determined to get their way. In 1884, they entered into litigation in the United States Federal Court in the Western District of Arkansas to dispute the legality of the town site title. It isn't difficult, at this juncture, to imagine Eureka Springs, which was rapidly becoming the best-known health resort in the nation, as an innocent maiden about to be plundered, like a defenseless victim, by big money interests.

The money due legal counsel to fight the lawsuit was $1,500, and the city treasury was bare. The state did not allow the issuance of bonds or tax increases. Sources of income were business licenses and fines. The city council was desperate. They begged citizens for donations. They issued warrants for 50 to 85 percent of face value. By April 1883, the city's outstanding debt was $78,816, and income was $36,679.

In 2010, City Clerk Mary Jean Sell wrote a report prepared for the mayor to settle yet another question of who owned the land under city streets. In her work entitled "Establishing the City of Eureka Springs, Arkansas 1880–1885," she gives a harrowing account of the financial situation from the minutes of the city council during those years.

It was decided that Mayor Carroll should go to Washington, D.C., to argue the case for the city's application for a town site with the determination that the land was mineral in character and since no minerals were discovered, the city had hope that it would receive its patent. However, as mentioned, the city treasury was bare. In order to get money to pay for the mayor's trip to Washington and to hire lawyers, the city decided to ask city lot owners to "pay such sums of money as they may be willing to advance," and that money would entitle them to a deed to the land when the suit was settled. Apparently, that plea didn't receive much response. On June 5, 1882, there was an urgent appeal for the citizens to come forward in response to the resolution.

On June 17, 1882, the council resolved that "each council member shall proceed to their ward and collect money to prosecute the town site case." By August 1882, the city offered that lot owners could buy quitclaim deeds to their lots at the price decided by the city (about twenty dollars per lot) and only have to pay half in currency. The rest could be paid in city script, which is not explained. This did not gain the desired result.

The attorneys who were due this money, a sum of $1,500, were, at the end of Ms. Sell's report on December 4, 1885, still owed this money. The total, by now, had grown to $2,800.76, including interest.

On February 16, 1885, an act of Congress deeded 320 acres to the City of Eureka Springs with authority to dispose of the land as it saw fit. Chester A. Arthur, president of the United States, signed the grant. On February 20, 1885, the Eureka Springs Land Act legitimized the establishment of Eureka Springs, Arkansas, City of the First Class—but it wasn't over.

Northcutt, Alexander and the Eureka Springs Improvement Company lawsuit in federal court was still pending. Eureka Springs had no hope of finding the money to fight the case. Mayor Carroll called a mass meeting of the citizens—by now weary of the fight—and the litigants to try to work out the dispute. Tempers were too frayed. Powell Clayton asked that the meeting be rescheduled for a month later. The second meeting with the Improvement Company lasted until 4:00 a.m., when agreement was finally reached.

This probably would not have happened between any men other than John Carroll and Powell Clayton. Both were seasoned politicians, experienced in state government. They spoke the same language, and they both were astute negotiators.

We'll never know what went on in those five hours, but it could be that Clayton and his group realized that if they were going to develop the town and make the fortunes they envisioned, they couldn't do it without the goodwill of the residents. Eureka Springs won the right to proceed as a city, and the ESIC was granted franchises to establish a gas works, an electric company and an electric street railway. Clearly, Clayton's group was granted a lot of power, which didn't sit well with many of the local citizens.

Eureka's people were a different kind of folk. None of these people had been born here. They all had to endure extreme hardships to get here, and when they finally made it, the struggle provided a common bond. They became very territorial and protective of their bit of property. No big city outsiders were going to come here and take over what they had fought so hard to gain.

This spirit prevails today. Eureka Springs' culture is entirely different from rural southern, where family and blood relationships matter above all else. The city provides a refuge from the outside world, attracting a widely diverse population, where bonds of friendship are not a matter of blood or genetics but of the shared experiences. Eureka Springs is regarded by the rest of the county and the state with a degree of trepidation. They never know what the town might be up to next.

Charles A. Cutter, in his 1884 *Cutter's Guide to Eureka Springs*, describes the situation this way:

> *When the first excitement was at its height, everybody thought that if they could only secure a lot by building on it, their future was made. This crazy excitement was, in many respects, a detriment to the city. It brought a class of people who were of no advantage to the place, to say the least.*
>
> *Most of those went home by 1884 and the city settled to a life of peace and order.*

When the citizens approved the settlement of the land question, Eureka Springs was ready to fulfill its destiny as the queen of health resorts. It was time for the next phase of development and the entrance of Powell Clayton and his Eureka Springs Improvement Company.

Powell Clayton
and the Eureka Springs
Improvement Company

The present population is estimated at between 4,000 to 8,000. The principal business is to provide in some way for the entertainment of a visiting population. Therefore, if Eureka Springs will prepare for the accommodation of 10,000 visitors, extend to them a cordial invitation with the assurance of a hearty welcome and good entertainment, that many can be induced to come here at that time during the favorite season, and Eureka will be made a beautiful hill-and-valley city of ten thousand inhabitants.
—*L.J. Kalklosch,* The Complete History of Eureka Springs, *1881*

There was never any doubt about Eureka Springs' destiny as a tourist town. By 1881, when Powell Clayton moved his family to Eureka Springs, its fame as a health resort was assured. Newspaper reports at the time speculated that during a single summer season, possibly fifteen thousand tourists arrived to "take the waters."

Clayton was not only a master organizer and a skilled politician; he was also a very astute businessman, an entrepreneur whose ability to find business opportunities around him attracted investors. He never had trouble finding money to finance his ventures. His reputation for being ruthless in his dealings during his term as governor (1868–71) made him one of the most hated and admired men in Arkansas, particularly because of his violent eradication of the Ku Klux Klan.

Powell Clayton as a Union army officer. *Courtesy of the Cornerstone Bank Collection.*

Born and raised in Pennsylvania and educated as an engineer in Delaware, he moved to Kansas at the age of twenty-two, in 1855. Establishing a town where a railroad was planned was a common and profitable venture at the time, so he and four friends tried their hand at incorporating a small town north of Leavenworth. The town didn't succeed, but Clayton developed a vision of what a small town should be and brought these ideas with him to Eureka Springs.

He continued to prosper by investing in railroads because they were the most efficient means by which goods were moved in the country; horse and wagon was the only other method available. The friendships he formed with wealthy investors throughout the railway system would benefit him the rest of his life.

Clayton's military career began in 1861, when he became a captain in the Fifth Kansas Cavalry in the Union army. When he arrived in Arkansas in 1863 to participate in the Union army's occupation, he was a young colonel, well known for his "dash," his courage and his fiery temper. He repulsed a Confederate attack on Pine Bluff near the end of the war and was promoted to brigadier general in 1865. Military command responsibility shaped his personality into a decisive and forceful leader who expected to win at every turn. You were either with him or you were the enemy, an attitude he carried into business and politics. He found Arkansas a strange mix of Democrat and Whig, unionists and conservatives. Arkansas had seceded from the Union near the end of the war, and a new constitution was required for reentry. During the war, the northern half of the state was Republican and supported the Union. The southern half supported the Confederacy and was Democrat.

There was no Republican Party, but Clayton participated in a convention in Little Rock in 1867 and became a member of the newly formed Republican State Committee. Congress rejected the new constitution and declared the governments of Arkansas and nine other states illegal until they could come up with constitutions approved by Congress, granting equal voting rights to whites and freedmen.

Most of the delegates to the new convention in 1868 were Republicans because of what was called the "ironclad" oath, forbidding participation unless the delegate could swear that he had neither served in the Confederacy nor given aid and comfort to the enemy. That excluded nearly all the southern half of the state. This same oath applied to elections and probably contributed to Clayton's election as the first governor. Clayton became the Republican nominee for governor and became the first Republican governor of Arkansas in 1868, when the new state constitution, containing provisions required by Congress, was approved.

Arkansas was going through a period of unprecedented violence. The election of a Republican governor and Clayton's installation of a patronage system that excluded Democrats from political appointments enraged his opponents. They determined to overthrow the government by any means and sought the help of the Ku Klux Klan, which crossed over from Tennessee in 1868, encouraged by the state's largest newspaper, the *Arkansas Gazette*. Many regarded the Klan as a continuation of the war. It had the enthusiastic support of many southerners. The Klan's agenda was to kill Negroes and Republicans, and its members ran amuck, creating a reign of terror throughout the state. White politicians were murdered along with whole families of blacks, who were hanged in public to serve as a warning to those who would oppose the "cleansing."

Clayton retaliated in typical military mode. He recruited a militia force including a large contingent of blacks and declared martial law in ten counties. He instituted a vigorous policy of arrests, trials and executions that disrupted the Klan, decimating its ranks within four months. He restored peace to the citizens, sometimes by recruiting local posses. The Klan lost members because people were finally repulsed by the violence. When the rebellious counties promised to maintain order, he lifted martial law. Not everyone supported his methods. Many thought he declared martial law in order to increase his own power. The aftermath was to create a maelstrom of misinformation about Clayton's policies that would follow him the rest of his life.

After his term as governor, Clayton was elected to one term in the U.S. Senate, from 1871 to 1877—a period no less turbulent than his one as governor. He retired from public life and moved to Eureka Springs, where he had the time and the freedom to get on with his plans for developing the town.

Eureka Springs was ready for a man of vision. The town had expanded rapidly but without thought of what kind of town it wanted to be and what face it would present to the public. Clayton came from wealth. He was accustomed to going first class, and his vision for the town was that of a first class resort with beautiful people coming to enjoy the waters.

The number of tourists who made the difficult journey to Eureka Springs against all odds and enduring such hardship amazed him. The nearest railroad was at a town eighteen miles north in Seligman, Missouri. The St. Louis & San Francisco Railroad (the Frisco Line) came as far as Pierce City, Missouri, with plans to continue south to Texas. Eureka Springs was promoting the construction of a railroad, so the Frisco line, in 1880, built south from Pierce City to the town of Seligman. It was still a five-hour coach ride to Eureka.

Clearly, the first project had to be a passenger railroad. Clayton figured it wouldn't take much capital to continue the line to Eureka Springs, with plans to eventually continue on to Harrison. Since Clayton was president of both the Missouri and Arkansas portions of the proposed line, he lost no time in filing articles of consolidation, and a new company, the Eureka Springs Railway, came into being.

Clayton was also chairman of the Eureka Springs Improvement Company, which included two of his old army buddies—Logan Roots of Little Rock and Richard Kerens of St. Louis—and Arthur Foote, a railroad man from

St. Louis. These were all wealthy men with sizeable investments in railroads. Roots, Kerens, Clayton and Bernard Baer, of Fort Smith, along with the Frisco Railroad, became the common stockholders of the new Eureka Springs Railway Company. Kerens, who had become significantly wealthy in the overland mail and railroad businesses, was very active in Missouri politics and well connected. He was the largest stockholder and thus became president of the new company. Roots was principal stockholder of the First National Bank of Little Rock. Clayton was general manager of the project, and he got to work with characteristic speed. Because of the terrain, the engineering was difficult. By August 1882, work had progressed rapidly. A bridge had to be built across the White River. Tons of rock were blasted and earth was moved, hauled off by mules dragging buckets.

There is a story that reveals Clayton's typical methods of getting his own way. Right beyond the White River, a canyon had to be blasted through some rock. There was a house on top, and the owner was not about to grant a right of way

The new Eureka Springs and Northwest Arkansas Railway on its way to Eureka Springs. The tracks are gone, but some of the original engines are still at the train depot downtown. *Courtesy of the Cornerstone Bank Collection.*

to the railroad. He didn't want the noise and the smoke below him. Clayton parked a wood-burning engine right below the house and kept it running for days. Finally, the homeowner gave in, not being able to stand the stench.

By January 1883, the line was finished. Laborers worked through the night laying the last feet of track to the Eureka Springs depot site. On January 24, thousands turned out to welcome the first passenger train into Eureka. The residents were proud of their train. It became important in the social life of the town. Every year, on the Fourth of July, the population would fill the cars and be taken to the White River Bridge, where they would picnic all day and enjoy the river beach. There would be music, dancing and, after dark, fireworks.

The line was pronounced first class all the way. Through service from St. Louis by way of Pullman sleeper cars would follow in February. The fare, round trip, from Seligman to Eureka Springs was $3.50, and the one-way trip took an hour. The first phase of Clayton's plans for Eureka Springs was completed. It was time to move on.

There is one note of historical significance that is never mentioned in accounts of the railway. When the road was completed all the way to Harrison, Arkansas, to hook up with the eastern lines, it became part of a social movement called the "orphan trains." The trains came from New York, with a stop at Harrison before continuing on to Springdale, Arkansas, and points west. The trains were sponsored by the Children's Aid Society of New York and, although exact dates are not known, began running around the end of the Civil War. They continued until about 1929. The society worked with the foundling homes in New York City to try to place orphaned or abandoned children in family homes. Notices were published in each town before the arrival of the trains. One such notice appearing in the *Carroll County News* at the turn of the century guarantees that the "babies" arriving Saturday are quality children from orphanages and not children from the streets. Persons signed up for the program should come to pick up their child.

People working through foundling homes filled out forms detailing first and second choices as to sex, age, eye and hair color and ethnicity. At each stop on the train route, preapproved citizens selected as many children as they had signed up for from the ones on the train. Adoption was discouraged because the hope was that their real parents might want them sometime. Many of the children were actually indentured servants, the control of which was retained by the nuns working with the program in New York.

The orphan train movement began in response to a crisis of orphaned and abandoned children on the streets of New York City. Massive immigration between 1841 and 1860 brought more than four million people to the United States without money or jobs. Housing became a problem. The Civil War left a legacy of homeless children. When the orphan train movement began, it was estimated that thirty thousand abandoned children were living on the streets of New York. Two organizations, the Children's Aid Society and the New York Foundling Hospital, set out to help these children by starting a mass relocation program. Children from about age six to age fourteen were brought into the program and guaranteed they would have a home until they were eighteen. There were no records kept, but there is now an Orphan Train Heritage Society of America in Springdale, Arkansas, that will help survivors of this program in surrounding states locate their parental records.

The ESIC agenda was to build a first-class resort that would attract the refined, moneyed visitors from the east and north. By now the town was thriving, with more than fifty boardinghouses and hotels, bathhouses, churches and three newspapers. The first order of business, to make it easy for them to get here, had been accomplished by the new railroad. Next they

A view of downtown Eureka Springs before the great fire of 1888, which destroyed all these buildings, except the Perry House, *center*, Eureka's second-largest hotel after the Crescent, which opened in 1886. *Courtesy of the Cornerstone Bank Collection.*

would provide them with an elegant, luxurious place to stay that included all the amenities. The Perry House, next to Basin Spring, was the largest and best with one hundred rooms. There were other smaller hotels, but nothing would compare, it was said, to the fine edifice Clayton and his committee would build.

The story of this fabled hotel, and the ghosts still in residence, will be covered in another chapter. ESIC influence grew. In 1888, a disastrous fire took out a large section of Spring Street on both sides. Since there were no more large trees left standing, the rebuilding had to be done with stone. The committee bought a quarry near the town of Beaver, north of the city, on the White River, to profit from the demand. When a later fire finished the destruction of downtown in 1890, Clayton could finally build the kind of city he envisioned with elegant stone commercial structures. The buildings that make up Eureka's entire downtown commercial district were built after those two fires. They date from 1884 to 1907, when the Basin Park Hotel replaced the Perry House, Eureka's largest hotel until the Crescent was built.

An ample source of stone brought stonemasons to town. These were old-world craftsmen whose work can still be seen along the streets of Eureka. They

A view after the great fire of 1890, which destroyed all of Main Street from the Grand Central Hotel to the Spring Street intersection and both sides of Spring Street from the intersection uphill including the Flatiron Building. *Courtesy of the Cornerstone Bank Collection.*

knew how to lay stone without mortar, a method known as dry stacking, which is a lost art. Many of the walls still standing in the city are their work. The finest examples are on downtown Spring Street. Visitors view the massive stones used to build these walls with awe, wondering how men ever managed to move those behemoths. Throughout the residential area, miles of limestone walls hold back the mountain, protecting the cottages that have been built on scraps of land blasted out of the cliffs. One of the major activities of Eureka Springs Public Works is the never-ending repair of the 130-year-old crumbling infrastructure and the walls that occasionally yield to the pressures of major rain events.

When downtown growth needed room to expand, late in the 1890s, the masons built a series of arched bridges across Leatherwood Creek, running along Main Street. That stonework now supports parking lots between buildings on the first block of the street.

Amenities, in many cases ahead of their time for this area, are what made Eureka Springs a fabled resort. The compromise land agreement gave ESIC the right to operate streetcar lines and gas lines for fifty years. The Interstate Gas Company came into being in 1885, and in less than a year, gaslights lined the streets. Ten years later, Eureka Springs had the first telephone system in Carroll County.

In 1891, the Eureka Springs Electric Light and Street Railway Company was granted a franchise to construct a power plant to supply consumers. It took a few years, but Eureka had an electric transportation system to make getting around on the hills a lot easier, not to say convenient for the guests of the Crescent Hotel on top of the mountain.

Clayton was appointed to a board of commissioners to develop a water system. The springs supplied clear, pure water for those who could carry it or for bathhouses that were near a spring, but a dependable system was necessary to serve other needs of the population. By 1894, the legal paperwork and the issuance of bonds (by now legal in Arkansas) was accomplished to build a large lake reservoir and waterworks and install mains and fire plugs. The masonry dam and the limestone façade, completed in 1886, created a large reservoir that today is Bass Lake. It is a remarkable example of the stonemasons' art—a structure significant enough to be on the National Register of Historical Places.

Unfortunately, in the last three years, Eureka has had several once-in-a-hundred-years rain events that have applied enough pressure to threaten a breach and possible failure. The dam is beginning to crumble. When the present-day city council took up the matter of repair three years ago, it discovered not only that the plans for the construction of the dam had been lost in the intervening hundred years but also that no one remained who knew how to build that kind of dam. The council is still considering the matter.

Clayton, in his rush to achieve results, created a lot of controversy. His aggressive approach to any problem and his rapidly applied solutions simply didn't set well with the more laidback southerners. The feeling was that he and his Improvement Company had too much power and were going about things too fast.

Part of the problem might have been his personal manner. He came from wealth and naturally gravitated to those like him, which made those without his advantages feel that they were considered less important. His political style was elitist, which naturally rubbed the people who had less than he the wrong way. A more common approach might have given him more acceptance among the working class. Eureka's other astute politician, Claude Fuller, whom you'll meet in a later chapter, realized early on that a more earthy approach would yield more success. He delivered it to perfection.

Eureka Springs has always had opposing factions. The uptown chamber of commerce and the downtown merchants' associations, of which there have been many, have always disagreed. To this day, bitter political battles erupt every four years with the election of a mayor.

In the late 1800s, one civic group was promoting Eureka Springs' water and the privately owned water company was shipping it everywhere; another group complained about lost local revenue because of the water being shipped out and people coming into town to buy it without having to stay the night.

As business grew, Eureka Springs' culture of warring factions came into being. The Clayton supporters tended to do business with one another and get together socially. They lived mostly on the west side of town and on upper Spring Street. They came to be known as "Silk Stockings," so named because they represented the wealthier part of the business community.

At that time, the main business district was on Main Street. Business establishments, warehouses, hotels and shops lined the street from the Spring Street intersection all the way down to the train depot. The Grand Central

Left: Labels used by the Ozarka Water Company for shipping. *Courtesy of the Cornerstone Bank Collection.*

Below: Glass-lined tank cars ready to be filled with Ozarka water from Magnetic Spring. The water company was Eureka's largest business, shipping water throughout the continental United States. *Courtesy of the Cornerstone Bank Collection.*

Hotel and the Landaker House were here, and small shacks and modest housing covered the East Mountain Hillside. This group formed a coalition in opposition to the Silk Stockings and Clayton's group. They considered themselves the voice of the working class, and they formed a group and called themselves the Royal Order of Mohawks. The Mohawks stated their purpose as "opposed to rings, monopolies, trusts, and bossism at the local level." In other words: the Eureka Springs Improvement Company.

The previously mentioned territorially possessive attitude of some citizens and the fear that, somehow, "bigger interests" were taking over and leaving them out of the picture might have had something to do with it. The casual disregard the Silk Stockings showed toward the Mohawks might have fueled the fire. The die was cast for a culture of political opposition that continues to this day in various guises.

The problem seemed to be that Powell Clayton had most of the power and controlled most of the money. As hard as the Mohawks tried to unseat him from his position, they never succeeded. Thus began Eureka Springs' culture of "turf wars." There always will be a group perceived as having the power and a group that wants to usurp that power and gain control.

People who come to Eureka Springs for the first time marvel at the potential for it becoming a real jewel in the South and wonder why the town is so needy in so many things and why it hasn't grown. The reason is the opposition that almost any attempt to grow encounters from a group inclined to object to any new idea, because the minimal lifestyle they have developed sits comfortably with them and they fear change will take away what they have. They become a little frantic that the town will soon grow so much that they will lose their place or small piece of turf. Any demonstration of ability or competence in being able to get a job done is viewed with instant suspicion and the conviction of conspiracies afoot.

There is a story about a confrontation between the Mohawks and the Silk Stockings. One morning, plans were in place and work was to begin widening Spring Street. The Mohawks were riled up and assembled with guns, knives and anything else that might serve as a weapon, determined to stop the project. The leader of the Silk Stockings, Major True, seized a pick and marched into the crowd. The story goes that he turned his back to the rebels and said, "Assassinate me if you wish." In the nick of time, Clayton galloped down the mountainside with a rifle and pistol and shouted, "What the hell does this mean?" Major True finally convinced him to leave, after much shouting, and construction resumed. Another ordinary day in Eureka.

As time went on and Clayton's power increased both at home and on the political scene, the Mohawks festered in their discontent, raging against every endeavor that came to light. When Clayton left Eureka Springs to work on candidate William McKinley's campaign for president, and Major True left town, the dissent subsided, leaving behind a man named J.W. Newport, who had been a friend to both men.

Newport's claim to fame could be that of Eureka's first constant dissenter. He objected to everything, fanning the fires of discontent wherever he could. Various people have filled his role through the years, encouraging rumors of conspiracy among the group holding the power and fighting for victory at the ballot box. The problem with dissenters is that once they achieve power, they lose their voice. They don't know how to fix things, only complain about them.

Clayton's life in Eureka Springs garnered mixed reviews from some, but Eureka Springs was a better place because of his presence here. His solutions to civic problems—a kind of "damn the torpedoes, full speed ahead" approach—caused controversy, no doubt, but largely due to him the town had the railroad, a water system, electricity, gas-lighted streets and the Crescent Hotel. He brought class and style to Eureka Springs. Clayton was never a rich man, but he viewed life as an economic opportunity. He supplied the vision, the energy and the leadership, using investors to accomplish his goals.

After he left Eureka Springs in 1897 to serve prominently in the Republican Party, he never lost his dream for a greater Eureka Springs. He returned often, and in 1906, on his seventy-third birthday, the dignitaries in town gave him a celebration dinner at the Crescent Hotel. He was overcome with emotion and reiterated his dream that "Eureka Springs, one day, will be a magnificent city with beautiful drives and country clubs on a scale beyond belief."

Unfortunately, the contentious nature of the locals would continue to interfere with the city's progress up until the present day. Powell Clayton died in August 1914 and was laid to rest in Arlington National Cemetery.

THE CRESCENT HOTEL'S RISE, DEMISE AND RESURRECTION

The saga of Eureka Springs' Grand Old Lady, the Crescent Hotel, reads like a bad soap opera. Her birth was one of magnificent achievement and grandeur. Through the early 1900s, she thrived, only to fall on hard times, failure and obscurity as a college for women. An embarrassing period as a cancer hospital run by the infamous Dr. Baker was followed by several futile attempts at restoration. Finally, she acquired a benefactor who restored her as the grand hotel she was designed to be.

By 1884, Eureka Springs was well on the way to becoming America's premier resort town. It was time for Powell Clayton and the Eureka Springs Improvement Company to bring the next part of their dream to reality. Clayton wanted a world-class facility to rival anything in Europe. Never one to think small, he envisioned a castle sitting atop the mountain that would be visible from any part of the city. It would be five stories and built of the finest limestone available, which happened to be in the company quarry outside of town. The stone was of such density that it required specially qualified stonemasons to cut and fit it, so he brought them from Ireland to do the building. The walls of the Crescent are eighteen inches thick and set without mortar, a skill known as dry stacking. Those same Irish masons stayed around to build some of the massive walls still standing in the town after more than one hundred years.

Five stories and fireproof, Clayton decreed. It would have elevators, gas and a sewer system. There would be an incline railway built to the bottom of the hill, connecting visitors with Spring Street. The water supply would

The Crescent Hotel, designed by I.S. Taylor of St. Louis and considered a fine example of American Romanesque Revival architecture. *Courtesy of the Cornerstone Bank Collection.*

come from Crescent Spring, at the base of the mountain, but water from any spring would be available on request.

Strangely enough, considering the fame of Eureka Springs as a resort with healing waters, there was no provision for a bathhouse. Guests were taken to Sanitarium Lake, later named Lake Lucerne, for bathing. The basement, where a spa is now operating, was a bowling alley in 1886.

It was built at the cost of, by one accounting, $295,000 and, by another, $300,000. Translated into today's terms, those who can do the math would figure several million dollars.

Clayton must have envisioned something on the scale of Buckingham Palace, with a lot of French Chateau, Baroque and early Gothic styles thrown in. That's what his architect, Isaac Stockton Taylor, of St. Louis, Missouri, gave him: a limestone behemoth, a lonely queen sitting on top of the hill in all its overdone elegance, looking bizarrely out of place among barren hillsides, lacking a single tree, peppered with tacky, wooden buildings.

The intended purpose of this hotel was to accommodate the thousands of wealthy people who came here to take advantage of the curative waters. It was also built to provide a mountain retreat for wealthy railroad executives and their families. Coaches stood by to take the patrons to bathhouses in town or to Lake Lucerne for swimming. Horseback riding was very popular, and the Crescent had a fine stable.

No expense was spared on the interior, which has been restored to its early grandeur by the present owners. Modern amenities, like private bathrooms and air conditioning in the suites, still furnished in the Victorian style, have been added, but the spacious verandas, the gardens, the magnificent lobby with its pink marble fireplace and the Victorian antiques remain.

There is a poem written by Powell Clayton and carved into the marble over the fireplace. It's an oddly sentimental poem, typical of Victorian writing of the day, but surprising in that it comes from a man who doesn't reflect a sentimental nature in any of the biographies written about him.

> *Although, upon a summer's day*
> *You'll lightly turn from me away;*
> *When autumn leaves are scattered wide,*
> *You'll often linger by my side;*

The fireplace in the lobby of the Crescent Hotel, largely constructed of highly polished Eureka Springs marble. Massive marble slabs inlaid on the back have the names of the founders inscribed and a poem written by Powell Clayton. *Courtesy of the Cornerstone Bank Collection.*

But when the snow the earth doth cover,
Then you'll be my ardent lover.

Also in residence are the ghosts who have haunted the hotel from the beginning, but they are dealt with in another chapter.

The hotel was indeed a showplace with one hundred rooms, Edison lamps, steam heat, sewage disposal and an elevator. Although documentation is lost, it is expected that the management followed procedures familiar to the founders they experienced in the finer East Coast hotels. Verandas were

Early scene of the Crescent Hotel lobby showing gentlemen patrons relaxing. The reception desk is in the lobby today, which has been elegantly redone in late Victorian. *Courtesy of the Cornerstone Bank Collection.*

furnished with lounges, where guests could rest and imbibe mint juleps all day long. Water from their favorite spring was available all the time. Dinner was formal. Guests would gather in the lobby outside the dining room at the appointed hour, wearing all their finery, and wait for the dinner gong. They would file into the dining room, where the waiter assigned to them during their stay would seat them and bring their dinner, perhaps ordered ahead. The present-day hotel has on the menu Crabmeat Lorenzo, which was served at the grand opening.

Ah, the grand opening. The Eureka Springs Improvement Company spared no expense with this. Dignitaries from all over the country, accompanied by their wives, arrived, by rail, of course, and were carried to the Crescent from the depot in a classy Tally-Ho coach, seating thirty-five. The event was trumpeted in newspapers nationwide. Guest of honor and keynote speaker was the Honorable James Blaine, prominent Republican, U.S. senator and secretary of state.

When it came to ostentation, no one could outdo wealthy Victorian women. They attended laden with jewelry and wearing gowns of satin and lace adorned with diamonds sewn onto the fabric. The *St. Louis Globe* Society Page reported that the wife of Logan Root, a member, wore black velvet with a court train. A Mrs. Van Harten, whose lace gown was "sprinkled with daisies and diamonds," probably outdid her.

The hotel prospered through the Gay Nineties, although it never did gross up to the founders' expectations. Nevertheless, it enjoyed a period of prosperity along with the rest of the country, no doubt due to the prevailing peace. The United States had been without a major war since 1865, except for the Spanish-American War in May 1898, a skirmish lasting four months and largely credited to the instigation of William Randolph Hearst.

The years from 1908 foreshadowed a reverse in fortunes for the town and the hotel. Attitudes toward the effectiveness of the healing water changed when more advanced surgery and newer, effective medical treatments for disease were discovered. The traffic into Eureka declined, and the businesses left.

The Crescent was assigned a new role as part-time resort in the summer months and women's college the rest of the year. This arrangement continued until 1924, when the college was forced to close from lack of support. It had a brief revival in 1930 as Crescent Junior College but closed permanently in 1933.

The hotel operated sporadically under a host of owners until it finally went dark in 1937, when it was sold to Dr. Norman Baker. The ensuing period (which is explored in the next chapter) is the most bizarre in the history of the Crescent.

At the end of the "Baker Period," the Grand Old Lady underwent several changes of ownership with plans to restore it to its Victorian elegance, but the size and expense of the task proved to be too much for the succession of owners until 1997.

Marty and Elise Roenigk came to town from the east and bought the property, and finally, the Crescent had acquired owners who had the interest, the vision and the resources to do the job right. One of the most meaningful additions was a modern, fully equipped spa in the basement, which gave the Crescent the right to claim the title of "Destination Spa and Resort." Guests can now experience what it was like to stay in an elegant Victorian hotel, but with modern amenities.

It is said by enthusiastic local preservationists that the Great Depression saved Eureka Springs. The developers left, and there were no new replacements with the money to tear down the old buildings and build newer, modern ones. The more solidly built Victorian cottages with all the gingerbread trim remain to this day on West Mountain, around the Crescent. The downtown had been rebuilt with limestone after the great fires in the late 1800s, and those buildings are still standing and occupied with myriad shops and restaurants.

Making the turn off Highway 62, down the hill to the old section of town, is like entering a shift in time. The stone buildings, the narrow streets and the old stone sidewalks make it easy to forget where you came from and eager to enter another time.

Eureka Springs has attracted a lot of strange characters and some highly individual persons who give the town a unique character and a different look from other small towns. Indeed, the story is that one day in the 1980s, a Hollywood producer was out scouting locations for his film satire about an itinerant TV evangelist who creates a wildly funny, "happening" church in a backwoods town. He spent a day in Eureka Springs and was impressed with the, shall we say, eclectic appearance of some of the residents. Realizing he could save a bundle on importing extras by simply hiring the entire town, he brought his crew, put most of the town on the payroll and began filming *Pass*

Eureka Springs highway entry.

Downtown.

the Ammo, starring Tim Curry and Annie Potts. The film never made it big-time, but it is available on VHS. It was shown once, in Fayetteville, before going direct to video, and a local journalist reported that it was the only film she ever attended where the rolling cast credits at the end received a standing ovation. Veterans of the experience still talk about how those Hollywood people knew how to party.

All of which, in a roundabout way, brings us to Dr. Norman Baker and his cancer hospital at the Crescent Hotel.

THE BAKER YEARS
AT THE CRESCENT

Norman Baker was not a doctor. He was a charlatan and a scam artist of the worst sort who preyed on the desperate. He was the founder of the Baker Institute in Muscatine, Iowa, and claimed he had a cure for cancer.

This was only the latest of his profitable ventures. The man was an entrepreneur who could make money at almost anything. His talent for promotion cast P.T. Barnum in the shade. His career as a huckster began with "Madame Pearl Tangley," a mind reader whose show he produced with great success for about ten years. He then turned to manufacturing an air-driven calliope he invented, which made him wealthy. He opened an art school to teach drawing, although he couldn't draw. Another success.

In 1925, he built and owned a radio station, KTNT; the call letters stood for Know the Naked Truth, which gave him entry into the world of talk radio. Exercising his right of free speech to the outer limits, he railed against big business, organized medicine, aluminum and any prominent men he considered a threat. He became wildly popular and very influential, and even richer, but that wasn't enough.

He heard of a Dr. Charles Ozias who had claimed to cure cancer at his sanitarium in Kansas City. The "cure" was a liquid containing glycerin, carbolic acid and alcohol, mixed with a tea of watermelon seed, corn silk and clover. This cure you could either drink or use surgically by pouring it directly on the brain through a hole cut in the skull.

With plans to publicize a miracle, Baker recruited five volunteers from his radio audience and sent them to Dr. Ozias. Unfortunately, they all died, but Baker detailed their miraculous cure in a magazine he published.

In 1930, he opened the Baker Institute in Muscatine, using his radio popularity to lure hundreds seeking a cure for the disease. Outraged, the American Medical Association (AMA) launched an attack debunking his cure and demanding his radio license be withdrawn. Nothing they said had an effect, and Baker fought back with lawsuits and public ranting. He claimed that the AMA offered him $1 million for his cure to get it off the market. Business flourished even more.

Finally, in 1931, his radio license was revoked, forcing him off the air. The courts ruled against him in his lawsuit with the AMA, and a warrant was issued for his arrest. Baker left for Mexico, where he stayed until 1937, when he returned to Iowa to serve a one-day sentence for practicing medicine without a license. He then left for Arkansas, having been run out of Iowa, and bought an old, vacant hotel in Eureka Springs, Arkansas, named the Crescent.

As an affectation, Baker wore white suits and lavender ties. He had a fondness for the color purple and took to redecorating the lobby of the Grand Old Lady with a vengeance. He painted the entire room—walls, floors and stairs—purple, including the wonderful marble fireplace. His office off the lobby was purple adorned with machine guns, perhaps to discourage travelers from Iowa. Even Clayton's governor's suite, which he took as his own, did not escape. He used purple stationery and drove a purple automobile. Actually, his use of the color purple, or lavender, could have been by chance or simply dumb luck, because metaphysicists revere lavender as a healing color.

There are many stories, mostly unsubstantiated but with an element of credibility, about his two years at the Crescent—tales of terrible, painful experiments on patients. Some of the ghosts that now haunt the place are said to be wraiths that died during those procedures.

He was finally arrested by the federal government for using the mails to defraud and was sent to the Leavenworth Penitentiary in 1940 for four years. He never returned to Arkansas.

Typical of the classic sociopath, without conscience, Baker did not believe he ever did anything wrong, or at least, that was his public persona. Privately, he was heard to remark, as he left Leavenworth, "If I could keep my radio station open, I could make millions out of the suckers in the States."

Morris,
the Crescent Hotel Cat

One cannot write about the Crescent Hotel without telling the story of Morris, the Crescent Hotel cat, a domestic orange and white tabby in residence from 1973 until his death, at the age of twenty-one, in 1994. During his reign at the Crescent, he was the town's most famous resident, well known and adored by the tourists. His fans number among the thousands. At one time, he received stacks of mail, especially at Christmas.

Descendants of his progeny are everywhere in town. Morris had his own gene pool going at the Crescent. Many of the orange and white cats in town are clearly related, along with probably some of those in surrounding states, taken home by tourists.

He was a small abandoned kitten when he appeared in the basement laundry room of the hotel one day in 1973, when the facility had just reopened under new management. The staff fed him and named him, and he became the Crescent cat. Naturally curious, he followed staff members everywhere, but he never went into the rooms or the dining room. Morris was a very laidback, friendly cat who napped every afternoon in the hotel lobby and soon became a favorite of the guests, serving as official greeter from his place on the Victorian settee by the door.

There is a sign behind the lobby desk that has the name of the manager on duty. Morris had his own sign naming him general manager. His own special cat door was installed on the side of the building so he had access at

Morris.

the end of each season, when the hotel closed. A short flight of steps, built for him, made it easy to enter.

Visitors sent him Christmas cards and contributed to a "kitty treat" box the staff kept on the desk in the lobby.

Morris died in 1994 at the advanced age of twenty-one, but the hotel concierge still has visitors asking about him, and his portrait, with a framed eulogy, hangs in the lobby.

Eureka Springs loved Morris. His death made the front page of the local paper. More than fifty people turned out for his funeral in the garden of the Crescent. He had a specially made walnut casket with brass hinges, lined in red velvet. The priest from the Catholic church attended. The announcer of the local radio station read the eulogy, and several people spoke of their memories of Morris.

The ending to this tale can't be verified, but it's a good story. It seems that, just as Morris was being laid to rest, a tour bus pulled up to the hotel and discharged a load of passengers who went through the lobby and came onto the balcony overlooking the garden. When they stopped to view the proceedings, one lady said to another, "What are they doing? It looks like they're burying a baby in the backyard."

To which her friend replied, "Yeah. They do that in Arkansas."

Eulogy
In Memory of Morris...
The resident cat at the Crescent Hotel
Filled his position exceedingly well.
The General manager title he wore
Was printed right there on his office door!
He acted as greeter and sometimes as guide
Whatever his duties, he did them with pride.
He chose his own hours; he set his own pace.
The guests were impressed with his manners and grace.
Upstairs and down, he kept everything nice

Morris's headstone.

They might have ghosts, but they never had mice!
Due to the fact he was growing quite old,
He'd doze by the fire when the weather was cold.
His years were a dignified twenty-one
When last he retired, and his nine lives were done.
He filled his position exceedingly well,
The resident cat at the Crescent Hotel.
—Evelyn Robinson

Mystical Eureka Springs

E ureka Springs is a metaphysical place. There is a pervasive energy in the town that is experienced by those coming for their first visit, and they come back to have that feeling again and again. The most often-heard remark from guests, shopkeepers and innkeepers report, is something like, "I don't know what it is about this place, but the minute I get here I begin to feel better. There's just something here."

Since very early times, the Osage Indians knew something extraordinary was taking place. They considered this area sacred ground and would not get involved in any conflicts with other tribes in this area. Today, resident mystics believe that Eureka has several places holding a vortex, an area of whirling energy where one's mind, body and spirit can be aligned. The land around Grotto Spring is said to be a center of energy, as well as up by the Crescent Hotel, where there is a feeling of force emerging. There are other places near the springs where a sense of presence lingers from another time. It has been suggested that the intense emotion released by those praying for a cure has left a memory impression.

Travelers to historic sites where emotional events have occurred, like battlefields, are familiar with this. Some describe the sensation as a "place memory," areas where energy from past visitors simply lingers, and those whose minds are open to the idea can feel it. It is not unlike the sensations near the site of Pickett's charge at Gettysburg Battlefield or at Wounded Knee.

Is Eureka Springs haunted? Many residents think so, absolutely. Those who believe spirits have the ability to return from the beyond can recount paranormal experiences they've had. It requires an open mind and a willingness to explore ideas not readily accepted by mainstream thinking.

This might explain the orbs of light. You can encounter this phenomenon all over town, but especially at the Basin Park and the Crescent Hotel, if you have a digital camera with a flash and aim it at a dark place. You'll very likely capture some transparent balls floating in space.

Skeptics try to explain them as dust particles, but their appearance, the varying sizes and colors and their movement make the theory hard to accept. The more popular belief is that they are energy remaining from people who lived in that place but are without enough power or substance to have form. Strangely, some who have photographed them report that they disappear from the picture after a few months.

Manifestations are sometimes seen in Eureka Springs. They appear generally as mist without enough form to be recognizable. The film crews who come ghost hunting in Eureka Springs have caught some of these on camera. Ghosts have substance and form. They are the souls of deceased persons who have not passed on and linger, frequently from some unresolved emotional or violent experience. Sometimes they are trapped into replaying the event repeatedly.

The Crescent Hotel is probably one of the most famous haunted hotels in the United States. The spirit most often sighted there seems to be one of the stonemasons who worked on the building when it was under construction. He fell to his death from the roof to the second floor, near what is now room 218. This is where he hangs out, slamming doors, moving towels, sitting on the bed. Sometimes his hands come out of the mirrors. He's harmless but likes to play tricks. Room 218 is one of the most requested rooms in the hotel. He's a big favorite of the staff and is affectionately known as Michael.

The fourth floor has a lady who introduces herself as "Theodora" before she fades away. Dr. Baker is believed responsible for many of the noises coming from the basement, where the morgue was located. A ghost is sometimes seen pushing a gurney after 11:00 p.m. The legend is that some of the hapless victims are buried beneath the floor. The wraiths are thought to be cancer patients reliving the traumas of Dr. Baker's horrendous experiments.

Occasionally, in mid-October, a young woman will be seen on the balcony outside the fourth-floor lounge. She will leap from the balcony but always disappear before she hits the ground.

The hauntings are so taken for granted that the staff ignores them and the guests enjoy the novelty, although they're not amused by some of the antics going on in the dining room. Sometimes, late in the evening, Victorian couples will be seen dancing. Chairs and tables will be moved and papers scattered all over the floor.

The Basin Park Downtown, sister hotel to the Crescent, also reports that a child about six years old appears in the upstairs hallways when other children are present She wears a white dress with her hair tied in a bow.

The result of all this celebrity is an increase in the metaphysical activity in the town. There is a society that meets regularly, and psychics, palm readers, astrologers and tarot card readers are available. Shops that sell crystals, including the much sought-after stones from Mena, Arkansas, are found in the downtown area.

Eureka Springs is an unusual place, full of peace and possibilities.

THE SPRINGS AND BATHHOUSES

W hile thousands flocked to Eureka Springs in response to reports of miraculous cures achieved from drinking and bathing in the water, there were many who had doubts. What was in the water? How is it possible plain water could cure anything?

As early as 1881, skeptics were sending the water to respected laboratories all over the country looking for answers. The analysis was always the same: sodium chloride, magnesium chloride, magnesium sulphate, magnesium bicarbonate, calcium bicarbonate, aluminum oxide and a small amount of silica. Some of the springs varied in mineral content, with trace amounts of iron, but contained nothing unusual. Scientists all concluded that the water was remarkably pure and free of organic content. There was no doubt that bathing and drinking the spring water accomplished hundreds of cures.

A report from a St. Louis laboratory, Wright and Merrell, concluded, "The water is remarkable for its purity…the very small amount of solid matter held in solution renders it a powerful absorbent and remover of disease while the large amount of gasses contained build up the wasted tissues. The water is very similar to medical springs at Wiesbaden and Baden in Germany."

Different rock formations are what distinguished the Eureka spring water from others and made it special. The springs are replenished with rainwater that filters through six different types of rock strata before emerging into a spring. It is this intensive natural filtering that made the water so unique.

A local resident of the time, Dr. Johnson, disgusted by all the doubt, said, "The action of our waters in the cure of disease is well marked, and although opinions may be divided as to how they cure, all agree that they cure. Some may say that there is no virtue in medicinal waters and the cures are due to other causes. Then, we say, show us the other causes."

Indeed, one could wonder if the home location of the afflicted was making them sick, and a time spent bathing in and drinking clean water, with simple food, clean air, a lot of walking and sufficient rest, enabled their bodies to restore themselves.

On the other hand, perhaps they weren't testing for the right elements. After all, 500 million years ago Arkansas was under water and near the equator. When the Ozark Mountains rose out of the sea 300 million years ago, who knows what they brought with them from the ocean floor?

The Indians believed that the water from the healing spring was radioactive, although they didn't know the term. They claimed the water "brought fire from the flint" and could cure "pain in the bones." There is some truth here.

Magnetic Spring.

According to the January 17, 1919 issue of the local newspaper, the *Times-Echo*, chemical analysis using the latest equipment identified radium in the water of Basin Spring. It appears as gas. The standard for radium in water was 10.4 grams. Basin Spring water tested at 65.4 grams. The results were published in the Kansas City medical index, *Lancet*.

Magnetic Spring, right off north Main Street, was said to magnetize metal objects placed in the water. It became popular for healing nervous disorders, which isn't surprising, since electromagnetic healing was very popular in this country after the Civil War and even more so in England.

John Wesley, an Englishman credited as the founder of the Methodist Church, was also an acclaimed healer who advocated the use of electricity to heal. He promoted cold-water bathing but insisted that electricity could cure a host of diseases, including paralysis—an idea being researched today in the treatment of spinal cord injuries. In his book *Primitive Physick*, published in 1747, he claimed electricity was better than any medicine he knew. He also claimed that emotions have more to do with healing than most people will acknowledge. By the late 1800s, the use of magnets and electricity for healing had become very popular.

By 1882, there were reportedly thirty doctors practicing in the city, ready to advise health seekers in the proper way to go about using the water. There was even an Invalid's Association that met twice a month to hear testimony from those who experienced healing and offer counseling and group comfort.

The list of diseases cured by spring water was long enough to strain the credulity of the most devoted enthusiast. Among them were: scrofula, a serious tubercular infection of the skin; erysipelas; Bright's disease, a kidney disorder with pain, swelling and water retention; arthritis; rheumatism; gout; heart disease; dyspepsia; catarrh, which was a chronic nasal and sinus discharge with a foul odor; cancer; and something vaguely identified as "women's ailments," including disorders of adolescence, menopause and nervous exhaustion.

Cures were widely published in newspapers and books of the times. Excerpts from records in city archives from the 1800s tell the tale.

Reverend T.H. Jacobs of Knoxville, Iowa, testified that he suffered from paralysis (cause unknown). After nine months of bathing in Basin and Harding Springs, he was cured.

Mr. Sanford from Colorado, crippled and deformed, was cured in two months and opened a grocery store in town.

John Evans of Indiana had open sores on his body for forty years. The odor was so offensive no one could be near him. Constant bathing and drinking spring water cured him in four months.

J.E. Wadsworth, Esq., of Illinois complained of general debility and dropsy when he arrived in 1884. "Last March I went to the springs broken down and worn out from work, with a peculiar swelling in the lower extremities. At the end of six weeks I returned to my business feeling like a new man. To those who are worn out by the cares of business, or from the rigors of a western climate, I would say, 'Go to Eureka Springs.'"

Eureka Springs of Arkansas is a book written by W.W. Johnson, MD, and published in 1885. His work carefully documents stories of cures:

> *March 15, 1884. Miss Lizzie Kuchli, daughter of J.L. Kuchli, Minnesota, was brought here with a mass of scrofula sores, greatly emaciated, but by the use of the waters until August 18, 1884 made a complete cure.*
>
> *Miss Mary Field of Jerseyville, Illinois was blinded by Scarlet Fever at 2 months. Brought to Eureka Springs in November of 1880, and by February could see well out of one eye.*

Miss Emma Sinkins of St. Louis was cured in three months of chorea by bathing in Magnetic Springs. The cure that achieved the most fame is told on a bronze plaque at Harding Spring. It reads: "Twenty-year-old Jennie Cowan had been blind for seven years following a serious illness. She used the waters of Basin Park for seven months to no avail, and switched to Harding Spring exclusively. On August 22, 1880 her sight was restored, and her cry of 'I can see,' created a sensation among the visitors."

There is no doubt cures happened at the springs over time and with persistence. Certainly an argument can be made for mind over matter. Any doctor today will agree that attitude and a will to recover have a lot to do with healing. The springs were the last hope for many. Note that healing took many months. When penicillin was discovered in 1928, recovery time for many ailments was shortened to days, but even before then, traditional medicine was becoming more effective, and Eureka Springs was beginning a slow transition from healing resort to pleasure destination.

Sadly, today, the water is not usable for drinking or bathing because of contamination from broken sewer lines. The springs are self-cleaning because of the unusual rock strata, so if money is ever found to repair the lines, the springs will be clean again.

There are sixty-two springs within a one-mile radius of the center of town and forty-two within the city limits. The seven most famous are along Spring Street and can be seen by following the sidewalk from Basin Park to the Crescent Hotel. Each one is landscaped as a small park with benches and flowers, making them a favorite for picnics. The others are on East Mountain or hidden among the fissures in the limestone bluffs on which the town is built.

Eureka Springs is a small town, and most of the springs can be reached by following a map through neighborhood streets, past Victorian cottages set amid the urban forest that finally covered the denuded hillsides and turned the city green again. Begin the walk at Basin Park, where the spring that started it all is now under a fountain. The park is the social center of the town. On any afternoon, someone with an urge to sing might be performing in the band shell. Weekends become a meeting place for groups in town.

Basin Park.

Along the ledge by the back wall you'll find a commemorative sidewalk with personalized bricks, including two by Mike Huckabee, former governor of Arkansas, and his wife, Janet. People-watching is a favorite pastime in Eureka. Basin Park is the place to do it.

On up the hill and around the corner from the post office, you'll come to Sweet Spring. When Powell Clayton was laying out Spring Street, the spring was below the street, in the ravine. He had it moved to its present location. You'll see, behind the spring, one of the many stone stairs installed in early days as shortcuts to the street above. They're all public, so feel free to explore.

A block down, if Eureka had blocks, past the Palace Bath House, you'll find Harding Spring. Side note: Never try to go around the block in Eureka Springs to get back to where you started. None of the streets intersect, and you will get hopelessly lost. Now then, back to Harding Spring.

Look for the bronze plate that tells the story of the famous healing. This is a great place to sit and listen to the water. There are stairs here and a walking

Sweet Spring.

Harding Spring.

path at the top of the bluff that will take you to Prospect Street. Turn right and you'll come to the Crescent Hotel.

The street right next to Harding Spring, Howell Street, the one that goes straight up at what looks like a forty-five-degree angle, is closed off when it snows to provide a toboggan hill. The street is the site of the fondly remembered, sometimes annual, Halloween Pumpkin Roll. The story is that a marauding group would steal pumpkins from the front porches the day after Halloween. After dark, they'd roll them down Howell Street. Near the bottom, they'd go airborne when they hit a bump and land with a smash—great fun until the police got there.

Farther along, past gingerbread cottages turned into bed-and-breakfasts, you'll come to Crescent Spring, the original water supply to the Crescent Hotel. It was one of Eureka's most popular springs because of its landscaping, benches and streetlights. The lovely gazebo was built in 1885. The walking path behind the spring ends at St. Elizabeth's Church and the Crescent Hotel.

Harding Spring as it appeared in the 1880s. The houses are on Howell Street, by now a well-established residential neighborhood. These houses are there today. *Courtesy of the Cornerstone Bank Collection.*

View from Harding Spring.

Left: The view from Harding Spring in 1882 looking down Spring toward the future site of the Palace Bath House. *Courtesy of the Cornerstone Bank Collection.*

Below: Gazebo Spring.

The Carnegie Library is one of two remaining in Arkansas. There were 1,946 libraries built in the United States with Carnegie funds. Construction on the one in Eureka began in 1906 with a grant of $12,500 and was finished in 1912. *Courtesy of the Cornerstone Bank Collection.*

Right next to the spring is the Carnegie Library, completed in 1912, one of four in Arkansas built with funds supplied by a grant from Andrew Carnegie. It is one of the few remaining libraries still standing funded by Carnegie money. The interior décor holds on to its history. Though the reading table in the center of the small room may be cluttered with computers, there's still enough room for comfortable reading chairs on either side of the marble fireplace.

The last location on Spring Street before the road begins to climb up Crescent Grade to the hotel is Grotto Spring. It emerges from a cave in the middle of a beautifully landscaped spot on the street. This is the rumored location of one of the vortexes mystics claim give Eureka Springs its special energy and is one of the most peaceful spots in Eureka. From here, you can flag down the trolley and go up to the Crescent or back downtown.

The rock stratum in Carroll County is conducive to springs. It is estimated that there are some 1,200 here. In the city proper, most of the springs are on East Mountain, the other side of Main Street, and worth visiting, but driving

Grotto Spring.

would be easier. Begin at the intersection of Main and Spring Streets, by the Basin Park, and head under the bridge connecting Main with Spring Street.

At the Grand Central Hotel on Main Street, turn right and follow Flint to the top. Turn left and within two blocks you'll see Onyx, Carry Nation, Little Eureka and Cave Spring. Onyx (now Laundry Spring) is first, at the top of the hill. Because of its copious supply of water, it became a social center for families as they did laundry.

The water from Cave Spring won second prize at the St. Louis World's Fair in 1904 for the purest water, beat out only by a spring in Switzerland. The little lake that you barely see on the side of the road is Little Lake Eureka, made by damming the flow from several springs. It was the city's first water supply and swimming area for guests. The lake is now private property, but it used to be the site of Little Eureka Bath House, a favorite in the 1800s. Besides a bathhouse, there were concession stands and a platform for dancing.

At the top of Flint Street, if you turn the other way and then go straight a short distance on the gravel road, you'll come to Soldier Spring, at the

Laundry Spring.

Old Soldier Spring.

entrance to a small cave. Water from this spring was to have helped with pain from broken bones. There is a story here about how the spring got its name. It seems some bushwhackers, marauding bands sympathetic to the Southern cause during the Civil War, were in the area and attacked some Federal troops at the spring. Some fierce fighting broke out, and the soldiers won the skirmish.

When you go back to Main Street and go north toward the train depot, you will see the part of Eureka Springs' history that made us famous at the turn of the century. On the left is a round, stone house that was the site of the Eureka Springs Bottling Works, built by Powell Clayton and later owned by William Duncan. Here "Ozarka" water was bottled and shipped all over the country. The water came from Magnetic Spring, across the street on Magnetic Spring Road, and another spring, Bay, behind the train depot.

Ozarka Bottling Company had a contract with the Harvey System, famous for serving in dining cars on railroads in the United States. Ozarka water was served throughout the Midwest and on every Frisco Railroad dining car.

Roundhouse.

Four carloads were shipped to warehouses in Kansas City and St. Louis each week, and local sales were as brisk. It was the town's most successful business.

Characteristically, success was followed by controversy. A 1909 issue of the local paper, the *Flashlight*, reported that certain local citizens complained about the amount of water being shipped out of town. It was thought that, at least, individuals should have to come and stay a night to have access to the water.

THE BATHHOUSES

In the 1800s, indoor plumbing was not the order of the day, certainly not in Eureka Springs. Therapeutic bathing was available at thirty-five bathhouses built near the springs. They were plain, wooden buildings, nothing like our spas today, but they had bathtubs—the large, deep, claw-footed ones.

Cutter's Guide, 1880, reports that they all had male and female attendants. Patrons were offered hot and cold showers and a choice of douche, vapor

One of the earliest bathhouses in Eureka Springs. *Courtesy of the Cornerstone Bank Collection.*

or electric baths. That last suggests that Eureka Springs might have been following the teachings of John Wesley, the Methodist preacher mentioned earlier who advocated electricity for healing.

The *Guide* speaks highly of the Little Eureka Bath House, which offered a wide selection of specialty baths. One could choose from a plain bath, sea bath, sitz, Russian, electric, French bran or manipulation. Unfortunately, a more complete description of what each bath entails is no longer available.

After the turn of the century, when the popularity of hydrotherapy lost favor to more modern remedies, the bathhouses disappeared. Eureka Springs has rediscovered its heritage, and today modern spas with an elaborate selection of baths, massage, skin therapy and aromatherapy for pain and stress management are thriving.

The only bathhouse remaining from Victorian days is the Palace, on Spring Street by Sweet Spring. It was built in 1901 with elegant décor, luxurious suites and the latest in hydrotherapy equipment, installed in the

The Palace Bathhouse.

basement. The Palace still offers massage and some other services, and baths are still available in old-fashioned, deep tubs.

The unusual sign on the front came later. It's another one of those things never discussed in Eureka because its installation caused quite a bit of controversy, not only because it's the first neon sign west of the Mississippi River and not fittingly Victorian. It did the job for which it was intended a little too well. The story is that by 1920, the Palace had new owners and had become a thriving bordello. The management commissioned a flamboyant sign from France, using the new neon, to advertise the building's current activity. When the structure arrived in town by train, in 1930, a local artist known as "By Golly" was hired to paint it, and it was hung exactly as it is today. The ladies of Eureka Springs were outraged, and the visitors thought it a hoot. It still hangs in place today, unchanged, with the signature of the artist intact, but you won't find it mentioned in any tour guide.

The eccentric artist By Golly, shown with his ever-present donkey. He was a well-known character around town who painted the Palace Hotel bathhouse sign. His signature appears on the sign. *Courtesy of the Cornerstone Bank Collection.*

There is a Palace ghost, of course. She appears sometimes in Suite 4, wearing a white chiffon gown. She supposedly died in the throes of passion during the bordello days.

Considering that the very foundation of Eureka Springs was as a health resort where water played a major role, it seems odd that the Palace was the only operating bathhouse until the 1990s, when the New Moon Spa at the Crescent Hotel opened. In fact, the Palace was the only operating bathhouse in Arkansas north of Hot Springs.

CARRY A. NATION

Eureka Springs has always been a refuge for those seeking a time-out from the real world. The simple lifestyle maintained from earliest days, and the ready acceptance by the residents of anyone daring to be different, has always provided a safe haven for the walking wounded. The striking difference between the residents here and elsewhere is that it doesn't matter who you were or where you're from. Your new life begins the minute you walk into town.

No one personifies the need for safe haven more than Carry A. Nation, who arrived here in 1910, near the end of her life. She was born Carrie Moore, November 25, 1846, in Garrad County, Kentucky. Much is told about Carry's life as a prohibitionist—the axe-wielding smasher of taverns—but the story of what made her into one of the most talked-about women in the world is even more interesting.

She was well educated and a contemporary of Amelia Jenks Bloomer, who wanted every woman to wear pants; Emmeline Pankhurst, Elizabeth Cady Stanton and Susan B. Anthony of women's suffrage fame; Fanny Wright, who believed in free sex; Margaret Sanger of Planned Parenthood; and Sophie Bardine, who, many believe, was the inspiration for Karl Marx's Socialist movement.

Carrie was outrageous, opinionated and a thorn in many sides, but she was also a forceful woman who knew how to get things done in a hurry. No doubt

Although she was born Carrie, she changed her name to Carry when she married David Nation because she liked to think of herself as carrying a nation on her back. *Courtesy of the Cornerstone Bank Collection.*

that rush to accomplishment was part of her undoing because southern culture regards anything done in a hurry with suspicion. What is seldom acknowledged is how she turned a life of incredible tragedy, hardship and deprivation into one of personal triumph.

Her early life was one of comfort, raised by servants and slaves and surrounded by religious superstition. Eccentricity ran in the family. Her mother believed herself to be Queen Victoria and was treated as such, eventually dying in a Missouri state hospital for the insane. Locals referred to several of Carrie's aunts and uncles as "tetched in the head."

Rebellious, headstrong, spoiled by privilege and determined to have her own way, Carrie was twenty-one when she married Dr. Charles Gloyd, over the strong objections of her parents, but she prevailed. The union was a disaster. Her long period of misfortune had begun. She didn't realize she was marrying a hopeless alcoholic. Commenting later on her marriage, she said, "I did not find Dr. Gloyd the lover I had expected." As he blamed the Masonic lodge, to which he belonged, for his condition, she developed a lifelong hatred for the organization. When she became pregnant, she was obsessed with the idea that Gloyd's condition would scar her child.

Indeed, something went wrong with her daughter Charlien. In early childhood, she developed an ulcer in her mouth that ate through her cheek. The condition baffled doctors, and a frantic Carrie tried every cure, from submersion in swamp water to eye of newt. The condition worsened.

The child's right cheek fell away, exposing her jaw, and she almost died. Eventually, the ulcer healed but left a hole the size of a quarter and a case of lockjaw that lasted eight years. The efforts to effect a cure left the child mentally ill the rest of her life.

Carrie blamed herself. Charlien had been resisting attempts to instill religion into her soul, becoming very rebellious toward scripture study. In a fit of total frustration, the mother beseeched God to lay "terrible affliction" on her daughter, and the ulcer appeared shortly after.

When Dr. Gloyd died, leaving Carrie and Charlien in poverty, she sold everything and went to school to learn to be a teacher. Her combative nature was not ideal for employment, and she was fired from her first job. Impulsively, she decided that the only solution was to marry. Within a week she met David A. Nation, Civil War veteran and her next disaster.

Nation had three professions: editor, attorney and minister. He was a woeful failure at all three and decided to move the desperate family, which included Mother Gloyd and a stepdaughter, Lola Nation, to Texas and become a farmer. Well, his cotton field dried up, he lost all his plows and tools, eight of his nine horses died and his farmhand ran away. The family was desperate and starving. Nation abandoned them all and set off to become a lawyer again.

For a month, the family tried to get by on cornmeal and sweet potatoes. When things were at their worst, and they had fallen ill from malnutrition, Nation sent word that he needed money. Sick and desperate, Carrie made one meal of the last of the food, loaded the starving family into a buckboard and headed to town.

Sometimes when things are at their worst, help comes. An itinerant Irish ditch digger named Dunn took pity. Carrie had thought she might be able to run a rooming house, and there was an incredibly run-down, rat-infested, derelict building formerly known as the Columbia Hotel that caught her attention. Mr. Dunn gave her his last $3.50, and the family went into the hotel business.

There were people wanting to board, and another investment of ten dollars got things going. Carrie did all the cooking, dining room work and laundry for the hotel and the guests by herself. Mother Gloyd and Lola cleaned. Charlien helped where she could. Mr. Nation showed up and spent his days sitting behind a desk in the lobby.

The backbreaking work took its toll. Carrie began the descent into mental illness that would shadow the rest of her life. She had insomnia, became delusional and had lapses of memory. Her religious fervor escalated to the point where she was expelled from both the Episcopal and the Methodist churches. She wasn't allowed inside the doors.

Two bizarre happenings solidified her fanaticism. The land was suffering a terrible drought. She organized a religious revival meeting and was allowed into the Methodist church for the event. After some Bible-thumping preaching, the rains came that evening.

The other incident was a devastating fire that was roaring down the street toward the hotel. Carrie sat calmly in the lobby while the building next door burned to the ground, declaring that she had "God insurance." By some happenstance of nature, the fire stopped right there, and the hotel was saved.

David Nation, deciding he would try his hand as a preacher, uprooted the family and traveled to Medicine Lodge, Kansas. The First Christian Church was hardly ready for what came next. Carrie had found her niche and ran roughshod over David and his preaching, frequently supervising his performance during the service and slipping further into bizarre behavior that would make many doubt her hold on her sanity. There are good arguments for describing her life from then on as a frenzied dementia.

Her enthusiastic endorsement of the temperance movement was a sign of the times. It was the custom in the South for the day to begin with a glass of mint-flavored whiskey, followed by "Leven O'Clock Bitters," a mid-morning alcohol break. Men drank in taverns; women and children drank at home with tonics and elixirs. Whiskey was used to quiet crying babies, and rum was a cure for just about everything.

Growing public awareness of the problem of excess drinking led to the formation of the Woman's Christian Temperance Union in 1874. Within a few years, it became the largest organization in the United States, with chapters in almost every state. All that was needed was Carrie Nation. When she embarked on her campaign to rid the country of saloons, she changed her name, legally, to Carry A. Nation, a play on David's name, because she declared it was her destiny to carry the troubles of the nation on her back. Kiowa, Kansas, in 1900, was the scene of her smashing debut that made her world famous for the next ten years.

Hatchet Hall.

She enjoyed her notoriety and promoted herself at every opportunity. She had small wooden cutouts of a hatchet made, which she sold for five cents at her gatherings. She liked to boast that she had been incarcerated in every major jail in the United States and Europe.

When Carry retired to Eureka Springs in the spring of 1911, her health was failing. She had trouble, sometimes, finding the words she needed to complete sentences, but she still had her dreams. One of them was to establish a home for women abused by alcoholic husbands or family members. She bought a house on Steele Street, near downtown Eureka Springs, which was named Hatchet Hall. It still stands today as a private residence. Unfortunately, she only had another year of life to make good on her dream, but in characteristic style, she left her mark.

The tale is one of Eureka's favorite stories. The simple, two-story house she purchased was built right along the edge of the narrow street. She realized that it needed running water for the convenience of the female residents. Across the street, the limestone cliff rose a few feet from the road. Carry could hear water running behind the rock. She knew there was a spring there, but how would she access the water?

She found a few sticks of dynamite and blew a hole in the side of the cliff, and when she found water, she ran a pipe across the road and into the house. The spring, Carry A. Nation Spring, is still there today.

Carry suffered what was apparently a stroke while making a speech in Basin Park on January 13, 1910, and collapsed, whispering, "I have done what I could." She was taken to a hospital in Leavenworth, Kansas, where

Carry A. Nation enjoys water from her new spring. *Courtesy of the Cornerstone Bank Collection.*

she died five months later on June 2, 1911. She was buried next to her mother in Belton, Missouri, in an unmarked grave. Finally, in 1923, friends raised funds to erect a granite shaft bearing the legend:

> *Carry A. Nation*
> *Faithful to the cause of prohibition.*
> *"She Hath Done What She Could."*

CLAUDE FULLER, MASTER POLITICIAN

C laude Fuller, like Hugh Montgomery, Powell Clayton and John Carroll, personifies those very talented people showing up just when the town needed them to accomplish the early development of Eureka Springs. Considering the tremendous contributions he made to Eureka Springs during the various political offices he held, there is very little written about Fuller in local history books. The reasons for this are obscure, but it is time he got a fair hearing.

His entrance into politics in Eureka Springs and subsequent rise to prominence heralded a political change from the elitist style of Powell Clayton to the tough, down-home style of the backwoods politician. As the city grew, the population acquired a more diverse mix, gradually outnumbering the elite with simpler folk. Fuller's predecessors were mostly educated men coming from backgrounds that gave them the affluence and opportunity to achieve success.

In 1881, an article written by a reporter from the *Arkansas Gazette*, out of Little Rock, here to check out the burgeoning city, wrote of the pleasing appearance of the populace dressed in fine clothes of the latest fashion. He must have been looking at the tourists who came here every summer and stayed for several months.

The transition was similar to the change in national politics from the conservative patrician style of the nation's founders to the less refined approach of the Andrew Jackson era.

Claude Fuller. *Courtesy of the Cornerstone Bank Collection.*

Claude Fuller's plain talk and down-home demeanor resonated with his constituents. He wasn't born with this approach; he carefully cultivated it after observing and listening to the remarks of his peers. His style made him one of the savviest politicians of his era. To understand him, you must know from whence he came.

Background wasn't the entire story, of course. Eureka Springs was undergoing change. Any city experiencing such explosive growth brought many seeking to make their fortune. The town was fast developing an underbelly and had become wide open to crime and corruption.

Construction of the railroad and the hotels brought rough labor and a lot of unattached men looking for entertainment. With them came a rural Arkansas culture that commonly used murder to resolve an argument. Itinerants with no prospects and no visible means of support came because they'd heard there was money to be made or they had nowhere else to go. Some came intending to survive by their wits and any opportunity that came along. Saloons, lewd women and gambling appeared almost overnight.

One story told is about the Basin Park Hotel, after its completion in 1905. Some local ladies of the night, known as "door knockers," did a brisk business. When a gentleman checked in, it was customary for the traveler to hear a knock on the door and a female voice asking if the customer required entertainment for the evening.

A citizens' committee was formed to deal with such behavior. Unattached females were discouraged from residing in town by the more genteel of the ladies' societies, and some places of ill repute in town were shut down, only to reappear as roadhouses beyond the city limits.

It was into this changing environment that Maria and Wilmont Fuller brought their three young children, Claude, his brother Harvey and his sister Maude, to live about 1885. The Fullers had been homesteaders in Kansas, barely eking out a living in harsh conditions. Life was hard. Many nights the children went to bed hungry. Shelter was a minimal three-room shack with a cookstove.

Maria Fuller was a woman determined to do the best for her family. She saw to it that her children had religion and got what little schooling there was available, but education was hard to come by, even though the Arkansas legislature had established a public school system. It cost money to attend, and the Fuller family had none.

Claude was the eldest, born in 1876. By the age of eight, young Claude was walking behind a plow, frustrating, heavy work for a young boy too thin and too small, but no amount of toil could surmount the hardships of prairie life. When an August storm destroyed most of their corn crop, the desperately impoverished family was forced to leave. They headed for northwest Arkansas, an area that Maria had heard about where life was better.

Settling on land outside of Eureka Springs, they began to produce goods to sell to the city. For a while, the family had some security, until the house burned down and they lost everything again and had to move into town.

Everybody had to find work to survive. Twelve-year-old Claude's first job, with his brother Harvey, was plucking chickens at the Crescent Hotel. It paid eight dollars a month and all the gizzards they could carry. For the rest of his life, Claude could not stomach the thought of stewed gizzards.

He attended school in Eureka, but to afford the tuition, he had to become the school janitor. To pay for high school, he became a mule driver and water boy for the street railway, making his way to school as often as he could. All this poverty and deprivation did one thing for Claude, according to his biographer, Frank L. Beals, in his book *Backwoods Baron*. Claude resolved that he would have money. He was not going to be poor, no matter what it took.

In 1893, Claude, now seventeen, decided, after consideration of the profit potential, to become a lawyer. He had no money to pay for an education, but he determined that he would make his way to Chicago. The World's Fair was about to open, and chances were good that he could find work and make enough money to afford college.

He and three of his friends hitched a train ride on a boxcar filled with hogs and took off, arriving in Chicago smelling at least as bad as the hogs. It took him a year of working at anything he could find and saving all his money, but it was hard; even a boy as determined as Claude finally had to admit defeat. He headed home the same way he came, deciding he needed to graduate from high school, which he did in 1896 at the age of twenty.

In the late 1800s, a law degree was not required to practice law. All you had to do was pass the oral bar exam before the court. It was extremely difficult, but possible. He studied at a local office and worked at anything he could get until, in 1898, he passed the bar and, with determination born of years of struggle, set out to be the most successful lawyer in the county. His lack of formal education was evident in the way he answered the questions. A judge who participated in the hearing told him, "You know your law, but you don't know English. I advise you to study the subject well." This was advice Claude took to heart, and he became an eloquent speaker.

Attending every trial he could get, he became a familiar courtroom figure, which gave him an insight into juries. His strategy became that any jury could be won over if you knew everything about every juror. You must get to know them, be friends, know what they like and dislike and they will have confidence in you and vote your way. He won most of his cases tried before juries by making sure only his friends served. Claude Fuller, politician, was born. His method earned him great success as a prosecuting attorney and even greater success when he opened his own office and became attorney for the defense. His Carroll County practice grew because of his success.

One case, a murder trial, presents a clear picture of Fuller's pragmatic approach to getting what he wanted. This account is taken from Mr. Beals's book.

Arthur Shafer, fourteen years old, was being tried for the murder of his father. Mrs. Shafer's description of her marriage was a harrowing tale of cruelty, abuse and assault on her and her daughters by her husband. She had eleven children, the oldest being Arthur. They all had to work the fields from sunrise to dark while Mr. Shafer sat on the porch and watched. If they didn't work hard enough, they were beaten.

When Arthur arrived in court to testify, he was a pathetic sight, dressed in child's clothes too small for him and inappropriate for a boy his age. The prosecution roared its disapproval, accusing Fuller of trying to sway the jury; however, Arthur explained that he had no clothes of his own, so the local ladies from the Baptist church had given the clothes to him.

His testimony left no doubt that he shot his father after the man said he was going to kill them all after they were asleep. Arthur was clearly guilty of murder.

However, Fuller assembled twelve practicing physicians in the courtroom and to each one, on the stand, read a question in impassioned language. Considering the circumstances, did the boy know what he was doing and was he accountable for his acts? Each doctor stated that the boy was, at the time, insane. The jury deliberated about five minutes and returned a verdict of not guilty.

Rural Arkansas was rough and tough. Family feuds were the norm, and the populace didn't take murder all that seriously, especially if it was to avenge a family argument. Claude Fuller fit comfortably into this environment. His acquaintances and political contacts benefited him throughout his life, and he never stopped collecting them. The following is an example.

Tom Fancher was a defendant in a murder trial. He was accused of killing his brother-in-law, Hugh Ussery. The Fanchers were an influential family in Carroll County. An election didn't go by when one of them wasn't running for office.

The case was open and shut. Fancher had killed Ussery in cold blood while Ussery was unarmed. Tom Fancher was found guilty and sentenced to four years in the penitentiary; however, he never served a day of the sentence. Claude Fuller secured a pardon for him before he ever reached jail. A local description of a very smart and wily man is to say, "He's dumb like a fox."

Claude Fuller was so wily in his trial strategies that some of his cases would be humorous if they weren't so serious. Consider the case of A.J. Cox, age sixty-six, retired, with a wife and son Claude, twenty years of age. They had a maid named Millie, under sixteen. Millie had plans for Claude and followed him to St. Louis, but when she got there, she couldn't find him. When she came home, she sued A.J. for $30,000 for "Carnal Abuse of a Girl Under Sixteen." A serious jail offense usually decided for the plaintiff.

It looked hopeless, but Fuller went to work digging up every bit of information on the girl he could find. When it came to selecting the jury, Claude only accepted men who were sixty-five or over. When asked why, he replied, "I intend to introduce evidence that only men of mature years can evaluate."

The case went to trial. Millie took the stand, and Claude questioned her carefully. In answer to his question, she stated she had been intimate with Cox on four nights in succession and that on each occasion they had had intercourse four times. The reason for the old men became apparent.

Fuller called as a witness a man who had gone about with Millie. He testified that she told him that when she got her money from Cox she was going to Kansas City to open a house of prostitution that would be her life's work.

At this point Fuller rested his case, but the prosecution persisted, much to his regret. He demanded the witness relate the rest of the conversation. He quoted her as using vulgar and profane language, in the course of which she said, "I will never have intercourse with another blank, blank Arkansawyer." The jury took a few minutes to return a verdict of not guilty.

Fuller's ability to accept a situation and turn it to his advantage helped him when he became interested in politics. After two terms as Eureka Springs city clerk, he decided, in 1902, to run for the state legislature. Fuller was a Democrat and faced stiff opposition from the Republicans. Shortly before the election, he and his wife went to visit Powell Clayton, by now an old man but still a power in the Republican Party. Fuller reminded Clayton of his time as a kitchen boy at the Crescent and apparently left a good impression. On election day, Clayton appeared at the polls and announced loudly that he was voting for Fuller. It created a sensation. Unheard of. The Republican boss of the South voting Democrat. Fuller won by two hundred votes.

After he lost a bid for the state senate, Fuller came back to Eureka Springs and was elected mayor in 1906. As with most things in Eureka, there is a story about that. When Fuller was in the legislature, he had spearheaded the passage of a law requiring the Northwest Arkansas Railroad to fence the entire track between Eureka Springs and Harrison, at considerable expense to the railroad. The people had never asked for this, and the idea seemed to spring from Fuller's hostility to the railroad. Business had been declining, and the company could not afford the expense.

Local citizens, recalling this dispute, were afraid that Fuller's election might end any chance of securing the ES&NA Railroad Shops, a lucrative retail venture, at the depot. At the last minute, a Citizens ticket was formed in opposition to Fuller's Independent ticket, and the rumor was that they might win. Influential locals, including William Duncan, came out in support of Fuller. Remember the name. He appears later as the focal point of Eureka's greatest financial disaster.

The Fuller ticket won, and it didn't make any difference to the railroad. Eureka got a new depot and the shops, and Eureka got the mayor it needed for the time—a tough administrator who would bring order to a town overrun with saloons that had become notorious vice dens.

As a first order of business, he ordered one of the most notorious establishments raided and the proprietor and the eight girls working for him upstairs arrested. Two nights later, Claude and his brother Harvey escaped an assassination attempt by two men hired to kill him. Two days after that, the chief of police met the saloon owner on the street and beat him senseless. He left town with his women.

The Eureka Springs Train Depot for the Eureka Springs and North Arkansas Railway. The first depot was built of wood in 1898. This limestone building was finished in 1913. *Courtesy of the Cornerstone Bank Collection.*

The city needed a courthouse. Records were stored in a rented room. Fuller lobbied members of the Quorum Court, the county governing body in Arkansas presided over by a county judge, until he had the votes. The night before the vote, he discovered two of the members necessary for passage were going to be absent. That night, the Eureka Springs chief of police went out looking and, early the next morning, brought the two men into Berryville in custody. The vote to approve the appropriation was tied, but Judge Tom Fancher, a friend of Fuller, voted yes, and in 1908 Eureka Springs had a courthouse. Yes, the same Tom Fancher for whom Fuller had secured a pardon. The town had to kick in $2,500 to seal the deal, but it got deed to ownership of the bottom floor in return. The county still occupies the two top floors.

In 1907, shortly after Fuller was elected, a disaster occurred that is hardly spoken of in Eureka's history—another hidden memory. Eureka Springs' major bank, the Citizens, went into receivership and closed its doors. The town went into a state of shock and denial. William Duncan, a man who had been accepted into the community as one of their own, was president of the bank. He pledged that all local creditors would get their money, but that hardly softened the sense of betrayal.

Duncan had come to town some fifteen years ago, with apparent wealth, and had been welcomed immediately into the community. He served on boards and committees with Clayton and other respected businessmen. Following along after the Eureka Springs Improvement Company, he acquired ownership of much of the company's property. He owned the Ozarka Water Works, the electric company, the gas company, the electric railway and extensive real estate holdings. Things started to unravel when he acquired the Basin Park Hotel. His finances were strained beyond the limit of tolerance, and he began to borrow from one account to pay another and, finally, to pay bills with checks written with insufficient funds.

In the early 1900s, there were no regulatory agencies for banks. If you wanted to start a bank, you rented a space and hung out a sign that said "Bank," and people deposited money. It was as simple as that.

The original Citizens bank building is still on Spring Street. A retail store fills the space, but each October the site is used for a reenactment of Eureka's only bank robbery, where irate citizens shot and killed the entire gang of robbers. It was a moment of civic pride.

While an audit listed liabilities and assets, more revelations were disclosed. The bank was several thousand dollars in the hole. Even worse, out of more than a quarter million in deposits, the bank had loaned a mere $45,000, and $3,000 of that was to the editor of the *Times-Echo*.

Another $10,000 went to the Eureka Springs Water Company, owned by Duncan. There were overdrafts of $39,000 written by Duncan businesses, including the water company, the electric company and the Basin Park Hotel.

Local newspapers were divided in their attitude. The *Times-Echo* called Duncan Eureka's greatest benefactor. The *Flashlight* suggested he might be a crook, although in more genteel words. A few weeks later, the *Times-Echo* went into receivership.

By August, all the fixtures and the bank building had been sold. Mortgage holders foreclosed on the electric street railway, the citywide electric system, the power-generating plant, the opera house, the Summer Auditorium and the ice plant. The bottom line was that about $135,000 in claims was assigned to the newly organized Central Bank and maybe would eventually be paid. Some creditors received satisfaction, and some received no more than 25 percent of their claim.

Claude Fuller served as mayor from 1906 to 1910. He served again from 1920 to 1928, after which he was elected to Congress. In those last four years, he accomplished two things worthy of note. He got a bond issue passed for $75,000 to build a city auditorium, seating one thousand people. The building still stands, on Main Street, newly refurbished, acoustically excellent and an object of pride for the town. Many local events are staged there, as well as touring acts.

Until Fuller's last year in office, the streets of Eureka had never been paved. There wasn't enough money in the treasury, but Fuller was determined. He arranged a bond issue to be sold to local investors and raised $10,000. Five miles of streets, which had been gravel for fifty years, were paved with concrete for the first time: all of Main Street to the train depot and all of Spring Street to the Crescent Hotel.

The state had passed a law that permitted the Department of Transportation to build highways through a town if the town paid half. Fuller got the state to make Main Street part of Highway 23 and Spring Street designated as Highway 62B. As a final act, he got the state to redeem all the bonds, so the paving didn't cost the citizens anything.

Fuller had always dreamed of being elected to Congress, and in 1928, he had his chance. At that time, because the area had a large population, there were seven congressmen to represent the district. He campaigned hard, using every political lesson he had learned in the ensuing years. He connected with his audiences by speaking in their language. He told them what they wanted to hear and bonded with them.

Before every group of farmers, he would begin his speech by saying, "Claude Fuller, on a summer day, raked the meadow sweet with hay"—not an original line, but effective. He would tell them he always wanted to own a farm but he was too poor to buy one, but if elected, he would come back and buy one here. He quoted Shakespeare when required and reminisced about his days working as a bootblack.

The primary campaign was down and dirty, but Fuller ran a clean campaign while the other candidates threw mud at one another. Gradually, he won the respect of the press and the voters and won the nomination. He was elected to Congress in 1928 and served until 1939.

Claude Fuller's genius was building a political base. He was a prominent Democrat and never passed up a chance to help a fellow Democrat campaign. His friends usually won, and they were suitably grateful. The system ran by patronage. You worked a successful campaign for the party and you got to pick the favor you wanted.

He was a good friend to Franklin Roosevelt and often served as his right-hand man in Congress, which paved the way for an appointment to the Ways and Means Committee, the most powerful committee in Congress, with the exception of the Patronage Committee. It was during his tenure that Social Security was passed.

He procured more than $2 million for the University of Arkansas at Fayetteville and established a veterans' hospital in that town.

Fuller was a man of vision. He realized times were changing and northwest Arkansas would need more than it had for continued growth. He pushed through the Flood Control Act that led to building of dams, creating Greer's Ferry, Bull Shoals, Norfork, Tablerock and Beaver Lakes. The project not only took care of the rampant flooding on the White River but also provided scenic lakes maintained by the U.S. Army Corps of Engineers, which provided numerous tourism opportunities. Eureka Springs acquired the pristinely beautiful Beaver Lake, only ten miles out of town.

The automobile was changing tourism forever. While Eureka Springs was struggling to transition from a health spa to a pleasure destination, it was clear that new tourists would prefer to travel by auto. Passenger traffic on the railroad was declining as the public began its love affair with the automobile. Roads were needed. The road from Seligman to Eureka was a rutted wagon track, no better than it had been in 1885, and virtually impassable.

Claude Fuller proved again that he was a man ahead of his time. If the town was going to grow, a road was as necessary now as a railroad had been forty years earlier. A proper road would have to be blasted through limestone cliffs and required a sizeable labor force. It wasn't until his election to Congress in 1928 that he gained the political contacts he needed to accomplish the task.

In 1916, Fuller campaigned for Charles Brough in his quest to get elected governor of Arkansas. The campaign was successful. Brough won, and now it was time to call in a favor. There was money for material to build the road but none to pay for the labor-intensive task of picking a road through limestone bluffs. Convict labor, however, was available. Fuller suggested that a convict labor camp be built outside Eureka Springs to supply labor for the job. The only money spent would be for food. The governor was happy to comply.

There is, of course, a story. It seems that the convicts were so happy to be working in the mountains, in cool air, instead of in the delta cotton fields, that they policed themselves. No one tried to escape, for fear of ruining what they considered a good deal. One inmate did try to run off, but the inmates caught him and gave him a beating as a warning to others who might have the same idea.

Claude Fuller retired from Congress and returned to Eureka Springs. From 1930 until his death in 1968, he was president of the Bank of Eureka Springs, a position later filled by his grandson, John Fuller Cross, and still later by his great-grandson, Charles Cross. John has an office in the downtown branch of the bank, now called Cornerstone Bank, and he's always available to reminisce about his Grandfather Fuller.

Here is how he got things done. He had a tremendous personality. He connected with people. Growing up poor gave him the skill to communicate with all kinds of people. Some people can't speak the language. He could. He believed in meeting with his constituents. I'd trail along behind him

One of the guards who supervised convict labor that completed the road from Eureka Springs to Seligman. This view shows the primitive conditions of the housing provided, which, although minimal, was better than the workforce was used to when they worked in the cotton fields in the delta. *Courtesy of the Cornerstone Bank Collection.*

Cemetery.

when he went visiting in the county and watch him fit right in with old guys in overalls and simple farmers. They accepted him as one of theirs because he knew how to talk to them.

Congressmen, back in those days, had three times as much power as they have today. They appointed postmasters, which was an opportunity to build a political base. Postmasters had a lot of influence in the town, and they could turn out the vote. If your congressman said you were going to be postmaster, you were. Qualifications didn't matter.

After Roosevelt got elected, my grandfather was made chairman of the patronage committee, the most powerful position in Washington. He got jobs for everybody. He was accused of giving more jobs to Arkansas than anybody else. It was the Depression, you know, and people needed jobs.

People come in here from all over Arkansas looking for me and they ask if I'm Claude Fuller's grandson. They still remember that my granddad got someone in their family a job when times were bad.

Claude Fuller was laid to rest in the Eureka Springs City Cemetery.

THE GREAT EUREKA SPRINGS
BANK ROBBERY

There isn't a lot of crime in Eureka Springs. The local citizenry is very territorial about their town. They don't put up with outsiders coming here to commit mayhem, and the locals know better than to get too far out of line. Citizens don't worry too much about locking doors or getting mugged. There might be a group of teenagers embarking on some shoplifting, but it's short-lived.

Things are so crime-free that the report of the dispatch desk in the weekly newspaper is a favorite of tourists because they love to read the short comments.

> *3:09 a.m.—A tenant of an apartment complained that near-by tenants were loud and boisterous. An officer responded but the party had moved on by the time of his arrival.*
>
> *4:30 a.m.—Resident reported large bird making noise in a tree outside the house. When the officer arrived, the rooster was gone.*
>
> *5:39 a.m.—An alarmed citizen discovered an individual sleeping on her back porch. Officers arrested the subject for public intoxication.*

So when five men from Oklahoma arrived to rob a local bank one balmy day in September 1922, the response was immediate and the story was one of the most highly publicized and sensationalized stories in American journalism, covered in nearly every newspaper in the United States. It has to be the most bizarre episode in any town's history. Yellow journalism was the mode of the day, and newspapers not too faithful to the notion of accuracy in reporting had a field day with the story.

The *Wichita Eagle*, on September 30, 1922, in an over-the-top account of the event, reported that after the bandits had committed the crime and were headed for their car, "they realized they had made a mistake. They were in Arkansas! No helpless crowd of hopeless citizens stood agape while dashing bandits sailed right out of their ken like a meteor on a starry night."

Not satisfied with this hyperbole, the article continued, apparently making it up as the writer went along:

> *Two pedestrians on the way to visit a sick friend, saw what was going on and stepped inside the bank door in time to open battle with a few well directed bullets toward the bandit's vital organs.*
>
> *A lawyer in an office overhead said to his client, "Excuse me a moment," stepped in front of a window and put half a dozen bullets where they would do the most good. A dentist asked his patient to keep open wide please for just a moment, and rested his rifle on the window sill long enough to make sure that at least one of the bandits would fail to leave town that day.*
>
> *A school boy hurrying home for lunch whipped out his automatic and joined the attack.*

The account, which was picked up by newspapers all over the country, made it sound like everyone in town had a gun ready to use at any time. It's a comment on journalism of the time that nobody cared if it was true as long as it made a good story. The facts of the story, as well as they can be determined, are every bit as remarkable as the fabrication.

The *Tulsa World* opined, "There is but one successful cure for the atrocious practice some worthless citizens have of forcibly taking from other citizens the means of sustenance. That cure was administered in the orthodox fashion to a band of worthless citizens by the citizens of Eureka Springs Wednesday." In other words, three of the five robbers were shot dead and the other two wounded but sent to jail after recovery, and the local avengers were declared heroes.

It shouldn't be funny when there is a street massacre in the middle of the day, but the account of this robbery is like the Keystone Kops meet the Earp brothers at high noon. There is a hilarious accounting in a booklet written by locals Edwin Tolle and Kevin Hatfield titled "The Great Eureka Springs Bank Robbery," available at the Eureka Springs Museum. This story is taken from that book.

It was near the end of a successful tourist season in Eureka Springs and the beginning of the county fruit harvest. The local banks were rich with deposits. Bank robbery was common during the 1920s, and small towns were particularly vulnerable because the citizens didn't have the means to fight back—or so the five men camped along Leatherwood Creek on the edge of town thought.

Three of the men, the Price brothers and Cy Wilson, were ex-members of the notorious Henry Starr gang from Oklahoma. When Starr was killed in a robbery attempt in Harrison, Arkansas, the gang disbanded. These three were wanted by Oklahoma authorities in connection with a robbery of a bank in Muldrow, Oklahoma, and were suspects in the robbery of a bank in Everton, Arkansas. The Oklahoma Banker's Association had employed a detective agency to find the outlaws, and there was a substantial reward offered for information. John Cowan was a sharecropper from Oklahoma looking for better days. The fifth member, Mark Hendricks, a Cherokee Indian, had come onboard a few days ago. Not yet twenty-one, he was new and inexperienced.

Charlie Price had been in town the past few weeks playing poker and getting the lay of the land. He had a plan. He told the group the business section closed up shop and went home for dinner at exactly five minutes after twelve. The bank employees would be gone and the street deserted—the coast would be clear. They would enter the town the back way on Highway 62, drive down Spring Street to the downtown, where the bank was located, stop outside long enough to do the robbery and then take off up the hill to Highway 62 and on to Missouri. Hendricks would drive the car and keep the motor running. Before they retired, Price wound his watch to be sure of the time. Now, this is where a quirk of fate enters the picture. Somehow, in the winding of that watch, the time was moved forward an hour.

The targeted bank, the First National, was in a row of stone buildings on Spring Street, a few doors from the Basin Park Hotel. The location is now a gift shop. The other Bank of Eureka Springs was at the end of the block, uphill. Business was brisk at both banks. Their vault doors were open, as was the custom in those days. Cashier E.T. Smith, at the First National, had just finished with a customer. He looked up at the clock, which said 11:05, and greeted his next customers, the Price brothers. They were an hour early.

We can only guess why the brothers didn't look at the clock or wonder why the bank employees were still there. It was now or never. They pulled their guns and yelled, "Stick 'em up!"

Everybody did, but Smith pushed the alarm button by his cage that would alert three places with a piercing shriek: the office upstairs, the Basin Park Hotel clerk and the Bank of Eureka Springs, up the hill.

While Wilson stood guard, the Prices and Cowan emptied the vault into a canvas bag. The take was about $70,000. Suddenly, the phone rang. Fate scored another knock. They should have answered the phone. It was the clerk at the Basin Park, and he knew something was wrong when the phone went unanswered.

Within seconds, everyone on the street knew there was a robbery taking place. The cashier at the Bank of Eureka Springs, up the street, got his revolver, saw the confusion at the other bank, saw the car with the motor running and, figuring that it was a getaway car, fired at the tires. The car careened up on the sidewalk at the hotel, where three more citizens were blazing away with shotguns and pistols. Hendricks fell out of the car, badly wounded.

Meanwhile, back at the bank, George Price grabbed the moneybag and bolted for the door. As the Price brothers, followed by Wilson and Cowan, who had grabbed two cashiers as hostages, emerged from the bank, they saw the car was gone. George and Charlie Price panicked, shoved the hostages aside and ran across the street to a stone stairway leading down to Center Street. Wilson and Cowan followed. By the time they reached the stairs, the owner of the jewelry store came outside with his revolver, took aim at Wilson and shot him dead. Town Constable Homer Brittain arrived on the scene, saw George Price running with the canvas bag, yelled for him to halt and shot him in the head. By now, the street was filled with outraged townspeople with guns. Charlie Price and Cowan were caught in the crossfire.

Charlie Price went down with a dozen bullets in him and would die four days later. Cowan fell with a destroyed hip. It was over. Ten minutes after the attempted robbery, the bandits were out of action. Cy Wilson was dead. George Price, mortally wounded, died twenty minutes later on the way to the hospital with Hendricks and Cowan. It was reported that hundreds accompanied the bandits to the hospital. Hendricks and Cowan recovered from their wounds and were sentenced to the state penitentiary. Cy Wilson's body was never claimed, and he was buried in the city cemetery.

The First National Bank closed its doors in 1931, a victim of the Great Depression. The Bank of Eureka Springs, now the Cornerstone Bank, will celebrate its 100th birthday in 2012.

The great bank robbery stands out as the most exciting event in Eureka's history. The day after, the local paper published lurid pictures of dead bodies and the bloody wounded. The gun-wielding vigilantes basked in their celebrity for years. The foiled bank robbery is still celebrated every year at the annual Folk Festival, held every October for the last fifty years. A reenactment is staged downtown at the original site. Locals are recruited to play the part of robbers and townsfolk. Women dressed like flappers roam through the crowd of confused tourists, most of whom have no idea what is going on. An announcer explains the activity, and at five minutes after eleven o'clock, an antique Ford pulls up in front of the bank and the robbers get out. There's a lot of screaming, gunfire—with blanks—and within minutes there are dead and wounded robbers on the street. Eureka Springs has yet again lived a moment in history.

THE SURE POP OIL
COMPANY SCANDAL

This is one of those things Eureka Springs has conveniently forgotten. Bare fragments of the tale are mentioned in newspapers of the time, requiring patience to piece together the whole story. The idea of striking oil, the excitement of bringing in a gusher, has stirred the imagination of the public since the early days of the twentieth century. Oil riggers were glamorized by the film industry, and everyone dreamed of getting rich overnight by discovering black gold. Arkansas was no exception, and Eureka Springs had plenty of people willing to dream.

In 1921, oil was discovered in southern Arkansas at El Dorado, making the area a boomtown, attracting hundreds of workers and investors. The news carried all over the state, so it is understandable that the town might get caught up in the dream of striking it rich with an oil well. That's exactly what happened.

As rumors go, no one knows quite how this one got started, but it quickly took off. Prospectors had been wandering through town as early as 1916, speculating on the possibility of oil underground. Local newspapers would report pronouncements from various "experts" that this area seemed to be perfect for the discovery of oil. "Best geologic authorities," whatever that meant, were quoted as suggesting that all it would take was money for a sample well and investors would become rich with little effort.

Stories began to filter in from El Dorado. A local paper reported there was so much oil being pumped out of the ground that it had to be stored

A happy crowd of investors gathers to celebrate the digging of the new oil well with a town barbecue. *Courtesy of the Cornerstone Bank Collection.*

in lakes until tanks were built. Local citizens were excited by a story being circulated about three investors—a Dr. Busey, David Armstrong (a farmer) and a Chinese laundryman—who had some money. They went together and drilled a hole in Armstrong's land while the public laughed at them. The oil gushed out of the ground, and Armstrong refused an offer of $3 million for his land. The three became rich, although Wang Hin, the laundryman, continued to wash clothes.

The trading in land and leases, conducted at a furious pace, created millionaires overnight. The stories dazzled Eureka citizens. The town was ripe for an oil rush.

In May 1921, C.H. Harrison arrived in town from Texas. Word spread that he represented wealthy Texans who had money for exploration and a lot of expertise in locating likely oil deposits. He came here to promote the drilling of an oil well.

Just about every businessman in town wanted in on the deal, and $10,000 was raised to buy a tract of land. Harrison introduced a friend, Hugh A. Tucker, a geologist from Dallas, Texas, and reputed to be an expert on such things. He chose a location near town that he claimed showed "one of the best indications of oil" he had ever seen. There is no indication that this was ever questioned by any of the residents. In Eureka Springs, the definition of an "expert" has always been and still is "someone we've never heard of, from out of town." The land was purchased from the owner, Claude Fuller, mayor of Eureka Springs.

The Sure Pop Oil Company was born and immediately went about the business of selling leases. Everybody wanted to buy a share in the oil well. Certificates were issued for units, and everyone with ten dollars to invest bought shares. An examination of the certificate transferring ownership of the units reveals clearly that although Sure Pop Oil Company was not incorporated, there were one million units available with no par value.

In 1913, the State of Arkansas had passed a law referred to as the Blue Sky law. Concerned over the amount of fraud being visited upon Arkansans by investment schemes and phony stock certificates that had cost citizens, for the last twenty years, more than $100 million, the legislature acted to put an end to the scams. Before the sale of any certificates, securities or stocks, state officials were required to examine the prospectus for evidence of fraud. The bill was opposed by the Banker's Association and supported by the National Association of Attorneys General. There is no evidence that this was ever done in the Sure Pop matter or that the Sure Pop certificates had ever been vetted by the state.

One peculiar attitude that prevails in Eureka Springs is the ability of the population to overlook facts that might prove to be unpleasant. Rumors are fine, but facts get in the way.

On Tuesday, October 4, the fledgling company held a huge barbecue for the town at the site of the oil derrick. An estimated five hundred people attended. They were invited to inspect the equipment, the bit and all the cables and drills. Dignitaries, including Mayor Fuller, gave speeches, and the crowd was assured that the value of town property would increase with the drilling.

News came from an unknown source that at an oil-drilling operation near the town of Crane, in southern Missouri, thirty feet of oil-bearing sand was found. Crane was forty-five miles north of Eureka Springs. If there was oil in Missouri, why not Eureka Springs?

On Thursday, October 20, 1921, Sure Pop ran a large ad in the local *Times-Echo* newspaper:

PARTICULAR ATTENTION!!!
You had better buy your leases before the price gets beyond you.

Additional ad copy reads:

The sale of leases to the world and the general public all the way from Ohio to Texas has been large. Everybody seems to be interested in participating in the anticipated profits to be made by the inevitable increase in lease prices and values.

The residents of Eureka Springs and Seligman and the surrounding towns are to be congratulated on getting in so generously while the prices are low.

WE WANT TO IMPRESS UPON EVERYBODY THESE FACTS:

First: That we are going to drill this well in the best workmanship manner to the depth of 2500 feet and maybe 3500 feet unless gas or oil is found in paying amounts before that depth.

Second: That we are going to produce oil or gas from that well, if it is there, and our geologic brain says it should be there in tremendous quantity.

Considering these two facts, it is an inevitable conclusion that the price of our oil leases, as blocked out around the well, will greatly increase in value with the coming of the horde of "oil scouts," and "lease hounds," and speculators who pounce on a field at the first showing.

The residents of this vicinity and the general public can rest assured that the management is practicing and proposed to continue to practice the policy of open square and fair dealing in all its transactions, both as regards to the drilling operations and the sale of leases.

We will at all times keep the public informed fully of all developments, and the management will, at all times, answer fully any inquiry pertaining to any phase of the business.

Duly warned, the residents rushed to buy more leases. Adding to the excitement, the local paper printed a letter written by Colonel George Thompson, a "famous wild-catter," to the Sure Pop Company. It read, "Your location is great. Globules of oil in the water of wells, oil traces, and actual positive seepage in many places tend to confirm the suspicion that oil

The Sure Pop Oil Company derrick, circa 1921. For a brief period, it represented the dreams of a town caught up in the excitement of "oil fever." *Courtesy of the Cornerstone Bank Collection.*

in large paying quantities exists." Colonel Thompson visited the area and left after purchasing some land.

Drilling continued, and at a depth of 540 feet, fossil rock and sand "oil rainbows" were seen on the water brought to the surface.

In early November, Sure Pop took the remaining unsold leases off the market and indicated it had sold all remaining property to a New York investment group, Associated Bankers Investment Corporation. A Sure Pop employee, a Mr. Thompson, unknown but identified as Harrison's assistant, was said to have gone east to close the deal. Local investors were not concerned. If big money interests from the North put their money here, they must think it profitable.

The investment corporation took out newspaper ads urging investment at great returns. On December 17, an ad warned that all leases would be withdrawn from sale by 9:00 p.m. that evening. More people rushed to invest.

In January, the well reached 780 feet and found pockets of gas.

On July 31, one year after drilling began, the derrick was destroyed by fire. The company had no insurance.

C.H. Harrison left for Dallas, supposedly to buy another rig; however, he never returned. One fire or another has destroyed all newspapers from that time, so no record of what happened beyond this exists. Clearly, the dream of riches beyond imagining had ended.

The wonder of all this is that in combing through local newspapers of that time, there was never any question of the legitimacy of C.H. Harrison. No one questioned the legality of the certificates, and there was no apparent uproar over the outcome. Considering that Eureka Springs always has a dissenting group opposed to whatever idea is being pursued at the moment, where was this group? Were they so mesmerized by the oil dream that they were silenced? We'll never know.

THE TOWN IS BUILT

I magine building a housing development without first planning the street pattern. Simply build the houses, facing every which way, without a straight line passing through anywhere and accessed by paths wandering at random between them. Then lay out the streets. You'll get an idea of early Eureka Springs.

The town developed so rapidly that estimates of population growth in the year 1879 go as high as ten thousand residents. By 1881, Eureka Springs was the fourth-largest city in Arkansas. The first housing was as close to Basin Spring as possible, but that kind of population explosion demanded services, and Hugh Montgomery's first attempts at a street rapidly filled with commercial buildings.

In a town built mostly of wood, with wooden sidewalks, clearly the real and present danger was fire. Eureka Springs was no exception. The haphazard layout of streets, with passages too narrow to provide access to the simplest firefighting equipment, made destruction by fire inevitable. The town was poorly equipped to fight fire. As late as 1886, there were no steam- or hand-driven fire engines, no hose carts and a minimal water supply from a city lake. Things didn't improve much until about 1909, when a group of forty-eight volunteers manned three hose carts. There were, however, fire hydrants installed in 1884.

The first disastrous fire, in 1883, destroyed seventy-five houses over five acres on upper Spring Street. Once started, the fire was impossible to stop

An 1892 view of downtown before the fire of 1893 destroyed most of these wooden buildings. *Courtesy of the Cornerstone Bank Collection.*

Main Street on fire, March 1893. This massive fire destroyed both sides of Main Street, all of Center Street and the Spring Street intersection. Following on the heels of the fire of 1890, most of the downtown was lost. *Courtesy of the Cornerstone Bank Collection.*

Spring Street after the fire of 1893. There was nothing left. The town council passed an ordinance that all buildings downtown must be built of stone. The present buildings bear dates from 1894 and are all built of limestone from the quarries on the edge of town. *Courtesy of the Cornerstone Bank Collection.*

A 1900 view of Basin Park after the fire of 1893 destroyed Perry House Hotel on the future site of the Basin Park Hotel, built in 1905. Spring Street continues uphill. Center Street is straight ahead. Notice the streets are still gravel. *Courtesy of the Cornerstone Bank Collection.*

until it burned itself out. In 1888, fire raged from Sweet Spring all the way down Spring Street to the Perry House. By 1893, most of Center Street, both sides of Main, the Perry House (which stood on the lot where the Basin Park Hotel now stands) and the Flatiron Building were lost. Both sides of downtown Spring Street were lost in 1888. By then, a law had been passed that all downtown buildings must be built of stone. Cornices of the limestone buildings in this area all bear dates after 1886.

The Main Street, otherwise known as Mud Street because during periods of heavy rainfall mud would fill the street, ran along the bottom of the hill right along Leatherwood Creek, which still flows today as part of Eureka's underground. When more room was needed for expansion, platforms and bridges were built over the creek, and development continued on the other side. These were later reinforced with a series of stone arches that today support parking lots along the street.

The constant need to grade and rebuild Main Street led to the gradual rise of the street level until Claude Fuller finally managed to find enough

Mud Street intersection.

government money to pave the streets in 1929. Some of the early buildings along Main are entered on the second story. The street level is underground. The unused basement level of these buildings still has the store display windows looking out on the series of tunnels that connect the buildings.

"Underground Eureka" can be accessed today by taking a tour, beginning through an entrance on Main Street. It is possible to see the arches, tunnels and some of the storefronts. The basement of the New Orleans Hotel, on Spring Street, is another place where this is apparent. The same underground structure holds true for Spring Street, which was filled and graded many times.

Several of the downtown blocks are hollow underneath, with the street level of buildings on the downhill side being underground. When the level got too high at some places on Spring Street, stairs were built alongside the building, becoming a new street, thus giving the building two street addresses.

As more springs were discovered farther up the hill, a residential area began to form. The area from Harding Spring to the Crescent was known as "the Boulevard."

Spring/Main intersection.

Early view of Spring Street, known as "the Boulevard," showing a collection of Victorian houses decorated with ornate gingerbread. These houses were built following the fire of 1883, when seventy-five houses on upper Spring Street were destroyed. Most of the houses shown on this street have become bed-and-breakfasts. *Courtesy of the Cornerstone Bank Collection.*

The street is lined with small Victorian cottages, many now bed-and-breakfast inns, built in the late 1800s and meticulously restored. These display the finest remaining examples of gingerbread trim to be found in the United States. It was all done by one man, W.O. Perkins, who came to town in the 1890s with his woodworking tools and established a mill. He is largely responsible for the ornate spindle work seen all over town. The most elaborate example of his work is near Grotto Spring, a tour home known as Rosalie House.

A turn-of-the-century edition of the *Daily Times-Echo* stated, "We remember when Spring Street, now the principal thoroughfare of the city, was but an uphill road, so narrow that two ordinary wagons could hardly pass without danger of being overturned."

For devotees of middle-class Victorian architecture, Eureka Springs is a treasure-trove. Because most of the homes were built after the fires at the turn of the century, which was the height of the Victorian age, and were carefully preserved, they offer a wide sampling of genuine Victorian design. A tour map available at the local museum showcases twelve styles of homes,

Rosalie House.

beginning with the starkly simple 1850s National Folk, made of precision-milled lumber, box-like and symmetrical, square or turned posts on the front porch and conservative, with no spindle work. It looks like a plain farmhouse. Following is a list of the rest of the styles:

GOTHIC REVIVAL: 1840–1880. The gables soar with scrollwork, beveled porch posts, cantilevered windows and steep roofs. Doors and windows are arched. The house conveys a sense of importance.

QUEEN ANNE: 1880–1910. Likely to have bay windows or a round porch on one side. Lots of turrets, gables and spindle work. This style is always the grandest on the block.

SECOND EMPIRE: 1855–1885. Eureka Springs' example of this style is called Penn Castle, and indeed, the gabled Mansard roofs with wrought-iron embellishments, second-story porches, arched windows and entries and the stonework carry ostentation to new heights. This house belonged to Gerald L.K. Smith until his death.

ITALIANATE: 1840–1855. Popular elsewhere, but not in the South due to the Civil War and economic depression. Eureka has two buildings in this style. Hallmarks include tall, narrow windows, elaborate window crowns and lots of porches.

FOLK VICTORIAN: 1870–1910. The style most likely to have a lot of spindle work and ornate porches with turned posts and balustrades. This style and its subtypes are common in Eureka Springs. Many have become bed-and-breakfasts.

COLONIAL REVIVAL: 1880–1955. The style resembles houses built on the East Coast in the 1600s. Relatively free of ornamentation. The shape resembles a Dutch barn.

TUDOR: 1890–1940. Deceptively modern-looking, symmetrical, with steeply pitched roofs, front-facing gables, overhanging eaves and bay windows.

ITALIAN RENAISSANCE: 1890–1935. The Eureka Springs Courthouse is a fine example of this style.

RICHARDSONIAN ROMANESQUE: 1880–1900. The Crescent Hotel, which defies description, is in this style.

It is indeed appropriate that in 2005, the federal government designated Eureka Springs a National Treasure.

MAKING THE TRANSITION TO THE MODERN AGE

Part of Eureka Springs' hidden history came about with the invention of the Model T Ford. The stretch of Highway 62 running through the town is on the National Register of Historic Places because it is one of the few roads in America fortunate enough to have mid-century roadside culture intact. The old motor courts, restaurants, gas stations and attractions are as much a part of history as the downtown buildings. Built mostly in the 1930s, it is still a major thoroughfare. In northern Arkansas, it remains a two-lane highway through Eureka Springs, where it is a part of American history of the auto age.

Eureka Springs' mindset is in the past. Residents do not readily accept that time goes on and things change. The town has gone through two periods of severe decline because change in the outside world was not acknowledged or stubbornly ignored. Consider what happened at the turn of the century, when water therapy fell out of favor as new medical practices emerged. Spas were popular all over the world, but the town's bathhouses, instead of upgrading to luxury, spa-class service, simply closed. It wasn't until the 1990s, when the Crescent Hotel finally had a spa, that the town began to acknowledge its heritage.

The years of grandeur for the city were 1885 to 1910. Due to the determination and vision of Powell Clayton, the town grew from a jumble of shacks to an elegant spa with grand buildings, many built of limestone—prime examples of the masons' art. The town's leadership had seen to

Eureka Springs was gradually catching up to the auto tourism movement. This is another motor camp for travelers. Remnants of this camp still survive on Highway 62. *Courtesy of the Cornerstone Bank Collection.*

View from Spring Street up Howell Street toward the Crescent Hotel at top. To the right is the Catholic chapel built in 1909 by Richard Kerens. In the center is Crystal Terrace, one of the town's most noted Victorian homes. *Courtesy of the Cornerstone Bank Collection.*

it that a central public water supply, a sewer system, streets, sidewalks, streetlights, public transportation and a railroad were in place. In 1904, Eureka Springs had about five thousand permanent residents, more than twice the current population.

Businesses and services filled all the local needs. There were fourteen physicians, eighteen grocery stores, dentists, bakeries, dry good stores, milliners, tailors, photo studios and nine jewelry stores. There were two banks, livery stables, laundries and bookstores. Life in Eureka was comfortable, business was good, tourism thrived and the future looked bright.

However, nothing stays the same, and the local residents were not ready to accept that life could not continue without change. Some saw the future coming. In 1906, Claude Fuller, a man who could recognize trends, would become mayor and realize the need for future planning, but for the present, Eureka dozed in the sun.

At the turn of the century, there were two ways to travel: by railroad or by horse. Most tourists arrived in Eureka by train, but as interest in Eureka Springs' healing waters declined about 1910, so did the rail revenues from passengers and freight. Government regulation of freight rates hastened the decline, and the Great Depression of 1929 took passenger traffic down to the level of failure for Eureka's once great railway.

The failing railroad moved its maintenance shops to Harrison, taking with it one hundred jobs and resulting in closed businesses and boarded-up stores. Suddenly, there was no way to get to Eureka Springs. Auto tourism was new and expanding, but the town, with the exception of Claude Fuller, had not seen the change coming and needed to catch up.

Experimentation with steam-powered vehicles had been ongoing in Europe since the late 1700s, but nothing practical was developed until 1885, when Karl Benz built the first modern auto in France. Generally, these vehicles were not taken seriously until Bertha Benz, his wife, took a road trip in 1888 in one of her husband's vehicles to demonstrate its possibilities, and man's passion for the automobile was born.

Let's leap forward to 1914 in Detroit, Michigan, where Henry Ford entered the scene with the introduction of the mass-produced Model T. Auto travel, overnight, came within reach of the ordinary citizen. Ford's cars, produced at the rate of one every fifteen minutes, could be purchased with as little as four months of a worker's salary.

After 1920, millions of Model Ts were on the road, and highways, which were largely rutted gravel, began to improve. Eureka Springs' citizens realized that a new era of tourism was upon them and they needed new businesses to serve auto travelers. The town began to revive.

Although the roads were still mostly gravel, Highway 62, a transcontinental route beginning in Niagara, New York, and continuing to El Paso, Texas, was becoming a reality. On a state map in the first issue of *Arkansas Highways Magazine* in 1924, the road was listed as a "Proposed Primary Federal Aid Road." Fortunately, then-congressman Fuller was influential in making sure U.S. Highway 62 was routed across northern Arkansas and through Eureka Springs, including the part of the road to Seligman, Missouri, which convict labor had handpicked through limestone bluffs earlier. This stretch of road is sometimes referred to as the Jefferson Highway.

The road brought a lot of people to this relatively undeveloped part of the country, which had been resistant to development. Eureka Springs became a popular stop on the route and led to the revival of the area. Another road, Highway 23, locally known as the Pig Trail because of its curves and switchbacks, brought traffic from the south.

When first completed, Highway 62 was known as the Ozark Skyway or the Ozark Trail. Its history followed the pattern of many early roads, which, at the turn of the century, were not a necessity. Henry Ford changed all that. His Model T became a common sight all over the country. By 1922, there were an estimated 10.8 million cars on the road.

Although the development along Highway 62 has modern motels, there are still many of the old structures remaining and still operating. On Highway 62 West, outside Eureka Springs, there were opportunities to develop roadside attractions with parking. Gift shops lined the road; the White River offered cabins and fishing, boating and swimming. Lake Leatherwood, a WPA project built in the 1930s and now a city park, offered housekeeping cabins.

The town is fortunate that so many of the early accommodations to auto travelers remain. Camp Leath was the earliest auto camp for overnight stays. As it added features, it became Mount Air Camp, then Mount Air Cottages and then Mount Air Center. It has evolved into a modern motel, the Best Western Inn of the Ozarks, and, recognizing a trend, has Eureka's only convention center.

One of the earliest gas stations in Eureka Springs, circa 1930s. *Courtesy of the Cornerstone Bank Collection.*

Camp Leath, one of the earliest accommodations for auto tourists in Eureka Springs. It was where the Best Western Inn of the Ozarks now stands on Highway 62. *Courtesy of the Cornerstone Bank Collection.*

Preservationists have fought to preserve remnants of the Victorian Age—buildings and neighborhoods that were considered old and ugly in the modern 1960s. While these remnants are still at risk, there is, at least, a body of knowledge about their significance, history and care. However, now preservationists are confronting an even greater challenge—how to preserve the twentieth-century environment.

The recent past has been described as "history you pick out of your own life in your town." For something to be considered "historic" by the National Register, it must be fifty years old. That's 1961. This is especially a concern with roadside commercial development that evolved with the auto age. These structures have become endangered because they are considered old and ugly. Urban sprawl has erased whole categories of once common roadside essentials. Where can you go to see a diner, a filling station with a garage, a motor court?

The short drive through Eureka Springs on Route 62, following along the mountain ridge, although historic, gives no hint of the Victorian village lying below. To reach the old town, you turn off the highway and go downhill. The old town area is so hidden by the trees that the casual traveler sometimes doesn't realize it is there. Suddenly, the historic district appears at the bottom of the hill. It's like entering a time warp to another era.

THE GREAT PASSION PLAY

It has been mentioned before that what makes Eureka Springs different from most small towns in America is the tolerance of its citizens to other beliefs and lifestyles. Eureka Springs welcomes diversity. It doesn't matter where you're from, what you believe or how you choose to live, as long as those things don't do harm to someone else. Matters of sexual orientation, belief in the supernatural, religion, color, race or personal lifestyle are simply not issues. Because the town is in Arkansas, a state famous for conservative religious views, like the debate over whether creationism or evolution should be taught in schools, outsiders assume that Eureka Springs is devoutly, rigidly aligned with commonly accepted conservative religious beliefs. Nothing could be further from the truth.

There are plenty of churches in town, all thriving. The town is home to a large gay community, but the matter is not discussed. Nobody cares. This might explain how one of the most radical and infamous anti-Semitic and anti-Catholic personalities ever to come on the American scene, an avowed hate-monger, found a home and success here.

It was about 1963, when the town was in the worst economic slump in its history. World War II, the Depression and the lack of business opportunities had left the population, down to about 1,500, mired in poverty. The town was ready for someone with an idea to show up.

Two things happened at once. Plans were announced to build a massive dam, creating a huge lake on the edge of Eureka Springs. The plan was part of a federal flood control project promoted by Congressman Claude Fuller. It would create interest in land sales and provide a lot of jobs.

On the other side of town, someone was anonymously buying acreage for an unknown reason that suggested some plans for development. Townspeople didn't have to wait long to figure out what was going on. That year, Gerald L.K. Smith and his wife, Elna, moved to town, bought one of Eureka's historic homes, Penn Castle, and announced plans to build a religious theme park on this property on the edge of town. It would be called Five Sacred Projects, and the first order of business would be a massive statue, the *Christ of the Ozarks*. Smith's ultimate plan was to build an enduring legacy that would culminate in not only the statue but an outdoor drama depicting the last days of Christ. The park would also house one of the greatest repositories of rare Bibles in the world, a religious art gallery and a replica of the Holy Land.

Smith, although not known to most Eurekans, was a famous orator who raised bigotry to a new level. He was a close associate of Huey Long and an avid white supremacist. He founded the Christian Nationalist Crusade in St. Louis in 1942. Its purpose was to "preserve America as a Christian nation being conscious of a highly organized campaign to substitute Jewish tradition for Christian tradition." Its purpose was also to oppose Communism, immigration and world government and to fight "mongrelization and all attempts to force the intermixture of the black and white races." It was a political party that promoted anti-Semitic and racist causes from the 1940s to the 1950s. It moved to Glendale, California, and was disbanded in 1977.

Smith was an enormously charismatic orator whom H.L. Mencken proclaimed "the greatest orator of them all, not the greatest by an inch or a foot or a yard or a mile, but the greatest by at least two light years." Considering the look of the man, six feet tall, over two hundred pounds, with a beak nose and intense blue eyes, it's not hard to imagine him holding a crowd spellbound.

His politics were somewhere far right of Attila the Hun, his beliefs were outrageously prejudiced and he was only peripherally concerned with the truth, but Eureka Springs didn't care. The matter had little to do with tourism and reviving the economics of the town. Eureka was a heartbeat away from dead and needed someone with ideas. Surely Gerald L.K. Smith was that man, although Eureka Springs did not comprehend the large scale of his ideas.

In January 1965, Charles Robertson, Smith's trusted assistant, announced plans to build a statue of Christ atop Magnetic Mountain on the edge of the town. The work would be visible for miles. Emmet Sullivan, who worked under Gutzon Borglum at Mount Rushmore, was hired to be the designer and project manager. "The statue," Smith declared, "would be more beautiful than Michelangelo's Jesus."

It is said that Smith had only $5,000 for the project at the end of 1963, but by the spring of 1964, he had raised $1 million to commission and construct the statue. It might be said that not only was Smith a great orator, but he was also a great persuader.

Work began immediately. The statue would be anchored in bedrock and built by hand with white mortar on a steel frame. When finished, it would weigh two million pounds and be sixty-seven feet tall, with a span from fingertip to fingertip of sixty-five feet. Each hand measured seven feet from the wrist. Components like the head and hands were constructed offsite. The head alone weighed seven tons.

The massive Christ of the Ozarks statue under construction. *Courtesy of the Cornerstone Bank Collection.*

There is, of course, a story. Construction of the statue involved thousands of pounds of mortar to be laid on the steel frame skeleton. In order to make the work go faster, Indians experienced in plastering were brought in from South Dakota, where they had worked on the Crazy Horse Project. The first day, the plastering went at a rapid pace. The second day, they began drinking on the job. That night, they went into town and got into a drunken brawl that landed them in jail. The next day, they were bailed out of jail and sent home to South Dakota.

The project attracted the attention of the media from all corners of the state. The statue was dedicated in June 1966. Claude Fuller gave a speech. It was viewed with a degree of awe and jealousy by the rest of the state. There were subtle suggestions that Eureka Springs had been chosen as the site for the project because the residents here would tolerate it better than elsewhere. An article in the *Arkansas Gazette* in May 1965 reported, with an almost audible sniff of disdain, that local citizens, though aware of the nature of the organization owning the project, were determined to know as little as possible. "The town is not picky about who promotes what."

Perhaps it was simply that the town knew a good thing when they saw it. Tourism increased. Thousands came to view the statue that sometimes defied description. The visitors needed food, a place to stay and souvenirs, all good for business.

Following his first success, Smith announced that there would be a passion play–type, outdoor drama, like that in Oberammergau, Germany, produced in a natural amphitheater in the side of the mountain. There would be seating for more than four thousand patrons. A stage, five hundred feet in length, would depict a street in Jerusalem, with numerous life-size structures such as houses, stores, a temple, Pontius Pilate's porch, King Herod's porch and a marketplace. The hill behind would provide settings for the tomb, Golgotha and the crucifixion. A tower would raise the Christ figure to a height of forty feet to depict the ascension.

To a town down on its luck, this was a miracle. Smith fueled their enthusiasm by visiting local organizations and describing what the project would mean to the town. He painted a picture of five nights a week when three thousand or more visitors would exit the play and descend on the town. They would need food and lodging and would stay to shop. With such a future in store, he advised people to buy land. It could only increase in price. The play would provide jobs for 250 actors, service personnel and animal wranglers, since real camels, horses, sheep and a donkey were going to be used.

His plans didn't stop there. When the play was up and running, he planned a Holy Land Tour, a Bible Museum and an art gallery. To support this project, the Elna M. Smith Foundation was announced as a separate organization sponsored by beneficiaries from all over the United States. Charles F. Robertson was announced as the chief coordinator.

The project he described was massive in scope and would require at least a few talented individuals to organize it. One of the assistants to the artist, Emmet Sullivan, was Adrian Forrette. He was a good friend of a producer, actor and director named Robert Hyde, who had experience in outdoor dramas and was looking for a project. With Forrette as the go-between, Hyde and Smith were introduced. Smith declared the meeting divine intervention as he became more impressed with Hyde's enthusiasm and ingenuity.

Hyde supervised the writing of a script, designed the original set, ordered costumes and made props. The plan was to use members of the community as actors in the drama, a sure way to get the cooperation of the town. It was a chance for extra money. The hours were good—evenings after regular jobs—and the job didn't require experience as an actor. To overcome the shortage and expense of professional talent, Hyde recorded the soundtrack with music and all the voices. It's hard to do justice to his monumental achievement in producing this play. He did it almost single-handedly. Again, it was a case of the right person showing up at the right time.

Construction of the stage and settings began in the summer of 1967. Smith publicized the project locally and nationally. News releases were sent out, including a sketch of the project and a description of the play.

Smith personally chose the site, a natural amphitheater framed on all sides by hills. Parts of the hillside would serve as locations out of the town, like Gethsemane. In honor of the site, the hill was named Mount Oberramagau. The stage and seating area were carved into the mountain with bulldozers.

The stage was constructed with multiple levels, the center being the temple, with massive steps strong enough to hold a crowd because most of the action was blocked around the steps and the temple. This was a major construction project meant to stand for years, so pillars of the temple had to be strong enough to hold a real roof made of lumber. Scaffolding was required for work to continue throughout the winter, and the set was nearly complete by the spring of 1968.

That May, production details were shared with the community, and a casting call went out. The entire town showed up at the Crescent Hotel— professionals like lawyers, business owners, cooks, waiters, store clerks and retirees. A local veterinarian, Dr. John Mueller, played an apostle, along with Floyd Miles, owner of a popular local attraction, Miles Musical Mountain Museum. The speaking parts were of the Sanhedrin, Peter, Paul and Mary. The disciples were major roles, much sought after. Their costumes were colorful and more elaborate than the hundred or so non-speaking extras who were the street people of Jerusalem.

There was something very appealing about more than one hundred community residents showing up night after night to perform a show for the tourists. Enthusiasm ran high as actors trained for roles. They were going to be paid, but not a lot.

There were two camels and a set of trained horses, which participants had to learn how to ride bareback. A small flock of sheep would run through town on cue. Several children, playing shepherds, had to learn to herd them. This was not as simple as it sounds, since sheep don't follow directions too well. There were several incidents requiring the herd to run from a pen on one side of the set to a pen on the other side, and instead, they took off up the hillside. The flight of doves was easier. They usually returned to their loft on cue. Those portraying Roman soldiers not only had to learn how to ride horses but also how to do it in awkward armor with weapons. They accomplished this all in a matter of weeks.

The set required a huge sound system. The one installed was state-of-the-art for the 1960s.

Robert Hyde played the role of Jesus Christ. He didn't plan to fill the role, but the Smiths were convinced that he was perfect for the part, so he played the character of Christ from 1968 to 1979. Since he was the one who would ride to the top of the forty-foot ascension tower, it could be considered an act of faith.

The staging of the play was an enormous logistical problem. The construction, costuming, training of animals and actors, acquiring of a support staff and recording of the soundtrack was all accomplished by the play's opening on July 14, 1968. It was a proud moment for the Smiths.

There were no other outdoor dramas in the country. Eureka Springs had accomplished the attraction that would pull it out of its depressed economic state.

Distinguished locals, members of the press and curious non-believers who couldn't imagine a town this small pulling off a project this large attended the first performance. One commentator was quoted as saying, "It is the greatest thing of its kind so far. In fact it is the only thing of its kind." It was for about twenty years, until other groups duplicated the project in other locations.

The opening night crowd was small, but its audience grew at a rate of twenty-five thousand per year. In a few years, it was the largest attended outdoor drama in America. It stimulated a building boom of larger motels in town. Restaurants large enough to accommodate the bus traffic opened along Highway 62. By 1976, the *Great Passion Play* welcomed its millionth visitor.

The play brought many new business opportunities to the town. In the 1970s, a change in the tax laws allowed accelerated depreciation of seven years on any historic home bought and renovated. Since the entire town had been placed on the National Register of Historic Places, every abandoned cottage in Eureka Springs was eligible for the credit. The change in the law sparked the beginning of the bed-and-breakfast lodging craze. By the 1990s, Eureka Springs had more bed-and-breakfasts than the San Francisco area of California.

The people associated with the *Great Passion Play* were welcomed into the community, and the dark history of the founders of the Elna M. Smith Foundation, owners of the entertainment complex, was never discussed. Charles Robertson served on the chamber of commerce board. The *Great Passion Play* organization had a member sitting on the City Advertising and Promotion Commission, and once again, Eureka Springs enjoyed a rebirth.

The nature of tourism is changing again, and typically, Eureka Springs hasn't quite caught up with the change. The *Great Passion Play* has been slow to realize that the attitudes of the masses toward religion have changed and a new point of view is perhaps called for. Attendance has been slipping. The economy has been affected by the worldwide depression.

What does the future hold? Somehow, someone will come to town with a new idea.

In the last few years, Eureka Springs has begun to rediscover its roots as an escape from the stress of real life to a healing place. Massage therapists have come to town. Several spas have opened, offering luxurious treatments to guests needing some relaxation and a little pampering. Restaurants have upgraded to cater to the more sophisticated tastes of their patrons; clothing stores are sought out for their unique "Eureka attitude," not to be found anywhere else. There is an increasing interest in things mystical. One can find psychics, palm readers and astrologers.

Near the end of 2011, in nearby Bentonville, Arkansas, Crystal Bridges Museum of American Art, with an $800 million endowment from the Walton Foundation, will open. This extraordinary wood and glass building, designed by world-renowned architect Moshe Safdie, will house the world's largest collection of American art from colonial to modern times. A 120-acre sculpture park and botanical garden will surround the building. The impact on Eureka Springs is already apparent, with the opening of new art galleries showing exciting new works by emerging artists.

Whatever happens, we'll be here, along with our ghosts.

Source Material

Arkansas Democrat Gazette.

Beals, Frank L. *Backwoods Baron.* Wheaton, IL: Morton Publishing Co., 1951.

Booth, Glenna. Eureka Springs Then and Now. Eurekaspringsthenandnow.com

Burnside, William H. *The Honorable Powell Clayton.* Conway: University of Central Arkansas Press, 1991.

Call, Cora Pinkley. *Eureka Springs, Arkansas—Stair-Step-Town.* North Little Rock, AR: Jenkins Enterprises, 1952.

Carroll County News.

Clayton, Powell. *The Aftermath of the Civil War in Arkansas.* New York: Neale Publishing Co., 1915.

The Crescent Hotel for the use of their various websites.

Cutter, Charles. *Cutter's Guide to the Eureka Springs of Arkansas.* Eureka Springs, AR, 1884.

Eureka Springs Times-Echo.

Fair, James R. *The North Arkansas Line.* Berkley, CA: Howell-North, 1969.

Flashlight.

Kalklosch, L.J. *The Healing Fountain.* Eureka Springs, AR, 1881.

Sell, Mary Jean. *Establishing the City of Eureka Springs, Arkansas—1880–1885.* N.p., n.d.

Taylor, Robert Lewis. *Vessel of Wrath: The Story of Carry A. Nation.* N.p., 1966.

Tolle, Ed, and Kevin Hatfield. *The Great Eureka Springs Bank Robbery.* Eureka Springs, AR, n.d.

———. *Sure Pop Oil Company Eureka Springs.* Eureka Springs, AR, n.d.

Westphal, June, and Catherine Osterhage. *A Fame Not Easily Forgotten.* Conway, AR, 1970. Eureka Springs, AR: Boian Books, 2010.

About the Author

Joyce Zeller is a longtime resident of Eureka Springs who has been involved in town matters for years. She's served five years on the city council, four years on the City Advertising and Promotion Commission and for a short time as interim marketing director.

This is her first published novel. One of her novellas, *Christmas for Annabel*, a holiday romance, is available as an e-book.

She is an aromatherapist and a perfumer and had a fragrance shop in Eureka Springs for thirty years. In real life, before coming to Eureka Springs, she wrote a weekly cooking column for a chain of suburban newspapers near Chicago, Illinois.

Visit us at
www.historypress.net